The Story of
LADIES' GOLF

STANLEY PAUL
London Sydney Auckland Johannesburg

The Story of
LADIES' GOLF

MALCOLM CRANE
Foreword by Belle Robertson MBE

TO PAT, EMMA, LAURA AND STEPHANIE

Stanley Paul & Co. Ltd

An imprint of Random Century Group

20 Vauxhall Bridge Road, London SW1V 2SA

Random Century Australia (Pty) Ltd
20 Alfred Street, Milson's Point, Sydney 2061

Random Century New Zealand Limited
PO Box 40-086, Glenfield, Auckland 10

Century Hutchinson South Africa (Pty) Ltd
PO Box 337, Bergvlei 2012, South Africa

First published 1991

Set in Goudy Old Style by SX Composing Ltd, Rayleigh, Essex

Printed and bound in Great Britain by Butler and Tanner Ltd, Frome, Somerset

A catalogue record for this book is available from the British Library

ISBN 0 09 174928 X

PREVIOUS PAGES: 1895 LGU Championship, Portrush.
Lady Margaret Scott putts.

Contents

Acknowledgements

Lady Amory, Jessie Anderson, Mrs Archer & Kenyan LGU, Diane Bailey, Elsie Bailey, Mr J Barclay, Canada, Karen Bednarski, John Behrend, Archie Baird, Jeanne Bisgood, Marjorie Buck, Tom Burton, Jane Carter, Canadian Ladies Golf Union, Mrs N Clark, Nancy Cook, Peter Crook & National Trust (Knightshayes Court), Helen Drake, Margaret Elliot, Mrs Val Cullen & New Zealand LGU, Jane Forrest, FFG, Ian Hatwell, Philomena Garvey, Joan Gray, John Graham, Janet Greenhalgh, Joan Hetherington, Norman Herron, Diane Henson, Pam Hirst, Irish Ladies Golf Union, Ann Irvin, Dr Leslie King (Canada), Ladies Golf Union, Laddie Lucas, Veteran Ladies Golf Association, Mrs S McKinnon (Royal Liverpool Ladies), Maureen Millar, J Miller, Wanda Morgan, Mr P Crook & National Trust, Tony Nickson, Anne Nottingham, Royal Liverpool Golf Club, Pau Golf Club, Maurice & Rita Osman, Betsy Rawls, Adrian Rickard, Belle Robertson, Royal Museum of Scotland, Mrs J Rothschild, Anne Sander, John Shiels, Marley Spearman, Davinia Sim, South African LGU, Swiss Golf Federation, P Taft, Chris & Liz Tetlow, Alan & Jean Thompson, Vicki Thomas, Mary Thornburn, John Tobin, Thelma Turner, USGA, LPGA, Adrian Walter, Enid Wilson, Eileen Winders, WPGET, Worplesdon Golf Club, and the good people of Singleton, Lancs and East Lothian.

Photographic acknowledgements
The author and publishers would like to thank the following who helped supply photographs or who gave permission for their use: Maureen Millar, Women Golfers Museum, Royal Museum of Scotland, Mrs Davinia Sim, Norma Clark of the Singleton Historical Society, Glyn Satterley, Hulton-Deutsch Collection, Phil Sheldon, AllSport, Mary Evans Picture Library, Popperfoto, Sport & General Press Agency and Peter Dazeley.

Foreword

I have had many privileges and honours during my long competitive career, most of them perhaps rather taken for granted, but on reading Malcolm Crane's *The Story of Ladies' Golf* I am greatly humbled. Perhaps such humility is a sign of my own advancing years, but if I have never quite appreciated the wonderful times that golf has given me – be it the everyday stroll round the course with friends or competing in the fierce cauldron of international competition – I do so now.

Issette Pearson, the first and only female member of the Wimbledon Club in 1886, made fantastic strides in the advancement of the game for ladies. Under her captaincy she began organising matches with other ladies' clubs and her appetite for golf and competition becomes clear. She formed the Ladies' Golf Union in 1893 and one wonders whether she would feel that the ladies' game had progressed satisfactorily since her day; she would undoubtedly feel exasperated with the women versus men membership disputes at certain clubs.

This book captures many facets of the game since its earliest inception and makes fascinating reading. I once had the honour of playing with the redoubtable Cecil Leitch and corresponded with her for many years, having gained her seal of approval, as it were, by winning a championship on her beloved links at Silloth.

Sadly my only contact with that great player Lady Heathcoat Amory, was when she presented the prizes at the British Ladies' Open at Wentworth in the seventies. I had read and heard much of this charming lady during my early years and I treasure the memories of that Wentworth afternoon.

The Story of Ladies' Golf takes the reader through the years with interest and humour and with very considerable insight into the comparatively new era of ladies' professional golf and its players. Expertly compiled, it is a thoroughly enjoyable book.

Belle Robertson.

Part One

1 Mysterious Origins

The origins of the game of golf are shrouded in some 500 years of Scotch Mist. It is true that medieval men and women played a variety of bat-and-ball games, but it is not really known which of these evolved into golf. Victorian historians thought that the game originated in the south of England, but many modern historians dismiss this. They think that golf was probably invented by the Dutch, and that the Scots subsequently fell in love with it, adopted it, and nationalised it in the 18th century.

Of the many continental sports of the Middle Ages, dozens of bat-and-ball games still survive, such as the ancient *Jeu de Mail*. This is played along French country lanes with a golf club and a wooden ball and bears a remarkable resemblance to golf. Perhaps it evolved from *kolven* or *cambuca*, or one of the other Western European games of the Middle Ages.

SPROUTING FEATHERS

Golf may be even older than this. The Romans had a club-and-ball sport called *paganica*, which used a soft leather ball stuffed with feathers. Now, most of us have heard of the famous 'feathery' golf ball that was used in the 18th century, and various experts have tried to prove a direct line from the Roman invention to this one. Unfortunately their theory ignores the fact that wooden golf balls were in fact used in the British game until gutta-percha provided a solid alternative.

Most of the early golf-like games that were recorded in medieval Europe also used a wooden ball, and the reason was simple. Feathers, even when they were bound with twine, were easily damaged. There is no doubt that the 14th century Dutch played a version of golf, called *colf*, with wooden balls on the frozen canals.

The Dutch, being a maritime nation, naturally thought in terms of wood because they used it all the time in shipbuilding. They had had trading links with other North Sea countries for centuries, and one regular port of call was Scotland, and in particular Edinburgh. They came to buy wool, for Scotland's rough pastures supported huge flocks of sheep, especially along the coastal 'linklands' of the eastern seaboard. By 1457 there are authentic references to the Dutch game of 'colf' being played around the Firth of Forth, and

the humble sheep kindly cropped the grass, so that the 'colfer's' ball could be quickly recovered.

Golf was, in those very early days, a simple game requiring the minimum of equipment. It was taken up by rich and poor and by men and women alike, although leisure and ample lawns and parklands were the prerogative of the well-to-do. Some lairds and nobles built their own private golf courses; the rest of the population used the rough sandy 'links' along the Firth of Forth seashore.

Archie Baird, the Scots golf historian, author of *Golf at Gullane*, produced a marvellous theory that rabbits provided suitable holes for golf in the links, and that their appetites kept the grass short. His theory cannot be just dismissed, after all, Archie is a veterinary surgeon.

From the 15th century onwards, the premier family of the region – the

Minchinhampton Ladies' Course 1890 by Lucian Davies of the Illustrated London News

Royal House of Stuart – were recorded as playing golf. It would appear that they were better golfers than politicians, as several lost their thrones and others their heads as well.

The honour of being the first recorded lady golfer did not belong to a Stuart. It went to one of their English cousins, the Tudors.

The second of the Tudor Kings was Henry VIII who had six wives. He had two beheaded and generally behaved like a marriage guidance councillor's nightmare. His first wife, Catharine of Aragon, managed to keep her head despite her husband's infidelity. Obviously she had little inkling of future problems when she wrote to Cardinal Wolsey that 'golfe kept her busy at court', whilst Henry was fighting in France. Perhaps if she had persuaded Henry to take up golf, the course of history would have been different.

Henry, for all his extra-marital activities, produced only one legitimate child who lived to a reasonable age. This was Elizabeth I. She did not play golf, but had many problems with history's second recorded lady golfer Mary Stuart, Queen of Scotland.

The entire Stuart Family had one major drawback as monarchs in that they genuinely believed that they had a direct line to the Almighty. Nowadays such a belief would be termed schizophrenia, but to the Stuarts it was 'Divine Right'. This belief of being answerable only to the Almighty may have accounted for Mary's questionable behaviour on the murder of her estranged husband James Darnley. She decided to play golf when the world expected her to mourn her late husband. Indeed, there was a strong suspicion that Mary may have played a part in his murder and ultimately cousin Elizabeth in London had to order her royal executioner to rid her crown of its Scottish thorn.

Elizabeth regretted the decision afterwards and nominated Mary's son, James VI of Scotland, as her successor to the English throne. In due course James moved to England and several of his loyal courtiers, knowing that his hobbies included golf, established the first golf course in England at Blackheath.

The playing of golf has been reported in England since the 14th century but it never had the popularity that it had north of Hadrian's Wall. By 1650 the game had even spread to Dutch America which eventually became a British Colony. Despite this princely acquisition, the Stuart Family's hold on the British crown had become increasingly weaker and in 1688, the Stuarts disappeared into exile, to be replaced by the Dutch Prince William. Sadly the golf course at Blackheath was not a major priority to the new monarchy, but a rare period of political stability in the middle of the 18th century saw the game at Blackheath re-established. It was to be a temporary respite. Trouble was looming throughout the land, in the shape of 'enclosures'.

THE ENCLOSURES ACT

Dramatic changes and improvements in agricultural efficiency were to make a huge impact on the lives of golfer and non-golfer alike. Before the 18th century, the modern concepts of secured land ownership and 'boundaries' were virtually unknown. Landowners and peasants were more concerned with husbanding the countryside than with fencing it off, and it was unthinkable that open land should be enclosed, or peasants turned off the commons. But with the arrival of new farm machinery, this is exactly what happened. Landowners became greedy and were obsessed with increased production. They therefore ejected labourers and smallholders from their land and left them to find work in the cities. It was hard, in such a climate, for golf to thrive among poor folk with nowhere to play.

The game was still mainly restricted to the eastern side of Scotland. But even there, the owners of common links land were suddenly concerned about their property being used without adequate control. This forced golfers to band together to run courses themselves, following the example of the

Honourable Company of Edinburgh Golfers and St Andrews Golf Society. Where once anyone could play over the links, now landowners sought assurances that users were maintaining the 'courses', as they came to be called.

A BLOW FOR WOMEN

The number of new golf clubs increased. The Industrial revolution and the emergence of the middle classes with leisure time and money to spend led to greater enthusiasm for sporting pastimes generally, and golf was to see an unprecedented growth in popularity. In 1800 only twenty golf clubs are known to have existed, playing over just twelve courses. Within half a century the number of clubs had trebled, but it was one of the old courses that struck a blow for women. Musselburgh, on 14th December, 1810, held the first recorded ladies' competition – for the local fishwives.

Despite this boost for the ladies' game, the vast majority of golfers were well-to-do Scots gentlemen, or Scottish soldiers, whose regiments had played a major part in the composition of the British army since the accession in England of James I. Scots officers were therefore to be found throughout the British Empire, and as a result golf clubs sprang up in India, Canada and Africa, all with Scottish names in their lists of founders.

St Andrews, 1889

Dr William Laidlaw-Purves, whose influence was crucial in the successful establishment of ladies' golf

Closer to home, in 1864, the Earl of Wemyss and a number of expatriate members of the Scottish Rifle Volunteers founded the 'London Scottish Golf Club' on Wimbledon Common. The same year, General Moncrieff of St Andrews persuaded his brother-in-law, the Rev. I H Gosset to found the North Devon Club at Westward Ho!, telling him it was 'designed by Providence for a golf links'. Nor were the female golf enthusiasts neglected. News came from St Andrews that a ladies' golf course had been finished, and that the home of the sport had now fittingly opened its doors to women, who were playing regularly. Following this example, Westward Ho! then established a ladies' course and the North Devon Ladies' Club was founded, on 8th June, 1868. The Rev. Gosset's daughter was on the committee and Mrs Hutchinson was president. This venerable woman was the aunt of Horace Hutchinson, golf's first great writer and a champion golfer.

These were the humble roots which developed into today's Women's game. The founding of the North Devon Club set the trend that was to rule ladies' golf, for better or worse, for many years to come; basically, if the club founders wanted their wives and daughters on the course or in the clubhouse, women were admitted. And if the elders did not want their womenfolk in the vicinity, then ladies were excluded ever after. And apart from Musselburgh, the great old Scottish golf clubs continued to exclude women. Many do to this day.

Fortunately, the London Scottish was not so unchivalrous, and on 6th April, 1872, the Wimbledon Ladies' Golf Club was formed, with fourteen members. It survived for seven years. The Earl of Wemyss and the London Scottish were having problems with some non-military male members, led by Dr Laidlaw-Purves. In 1881 a schism occurred which led to the formation of a new 'Wimbledon Golf Club'. Among the breakaways was one of London's most influential publishers whose daughter was showing a keen interest in golf. From 1886 onwards, he allowed her to play with him regularly. This young woman was responsible for taking the ladies' game by the scruff of the neck and making it into the game it is today. Her name was Issette Pearson.

In 1890 Miss Pearson began looking for a decent level of competition for herself and her Wimbledon teammates. She could not possibly have envisaged the changes she would bring to the sport in Britain, or to golf throughout the rest of the world where it was still in its infancy.

In America, the first golf club at Yonkers had one female member and was still using an apple tree as a coat hanger. In Australia, South Africa and New Zealand the first clubs had only just been founded.

The game was fairly well established in France, but when the summer season was over, the British golfers, both ladies and gentlemen, would pack their bags and head for home. The game then went into hibernation.

During the next twenty years, the rest of the world began to discover golf. And it was a girl who put the framework in place that women's (and men's) golf was to copy in every corner of the globe.

A brief history of the first 500 years of golf:

1300 Earliest mentions of *colf* in Holland.

1390 Public places in the Dutch city of Utrecht reserved for *kolfe*.

1457 James II of Scotland banned golf as it interfered with archery. Part of the old course at St Andrews was an archery practice ground in the middle ages.

1460 Golfers depicted in 'The Book of Hours' produced for the Duchess of Burgundy at Chantilly in France.

1500 Early paintings of *colf* in Holland.

1509 King Henry VIII's first wife Queen Catharine of Aragon wrote to Cardinal Wolsey that 'golfe' kept her occupied.

1565 The Aberdeen Register records that golf is now an unlawful amusement in the town and district.

1567 Mary, Queen of Scots was criticised for playing golf two days after the death of her husband Darnley. Mary subsequently lost her head more than temporarily.

1603 Dutch artist Aert van der Neer painted golf being played on frozen dykes.

1603 Mary, Queen of Scots' son James I of England (VI of Scotland) appointed his own clubmaker.

1608 Scots courtiers of James laid out a course at Blackheath but it subsequently fell into disuse.

1618 Scots ban on the import of golf balls from Holland.

1642 Charles I reported to be playing golf when news arrived of Irish rebellion. His head and body parted company seven years later.
Aberdeen Town Council granted John Dickson a licence to sell balls and clubs on the town links.

1650 Dutch artist Aelbert Culp painted a child playing golf.
In Albany, New York (then New Amsterdam), a Dutch court reports that persistent tavern brawler Jacob Jansz was arrested for using a golf club to inflict harm on a fellow drinker.
Annual New Year's Day golf match between the weavers of Dirleton and Aberlady began over Gullane links.

1658 Westminster School governors reported problems with vandals defacing the playing fields which interfered with golf.

1689 Thomas Kincaid of Edinburgh mentioned rules of golf in his diary.

1734 Reported export of golf clubs and balls from Scotland to Carolina, in the Americas.

1778 Bonnie Prince Charlie Stuart in exile in Italy is reported to have played regularly in Rome.

1743 The first recorded book on golf by Rev. Thomas Matheson of Brechin called 'the goff'. Originally costing 4d, a copy was sold at auction in 1986 for £17,000.

1744 Honourable Company of Edinburgh Golfers formed at Leith and introduced rules. After a brief sojourn at Musselburgh, the club moved to Muirfield.

1754 A group of worthies formed golf club at St Andrews.

1762 Report of golf club meeting at Bray near Dublin.

1786 South Carolina Golf Club formed in USA, but subsequently became defunct during 1812 War between USA and Britain.
(Royal) Blackheath was playing golf over 5 holes.

1810 Earliest recorded incidence of ladies' competitive golf at Musselburgh.

1818 Manchester Golf Club formed at Kersal Moor in Salford. Lost course later in century. The club is still in existence.

1829 (Royal) Calcutta Golf Club became first course in India.

1833 Perth Golfing Society received accolade of 'Royal' from King William VI.

1834 The Ancient Golf Club of St Andrews received the accolade of 'Royal'.

1851 First Continental course formed at Pau in South West France.

1854 Dirleton Castle Golf Club formed at Gullane on site of ancient golf course for the 'working classes'.

1858 R & A decreed 18 holes to be 'a round'.

1860 Men's Open Championship inaugurated at Prestwick.

1864 (Royal) North Devon Golf Club at Westward Ho!, and Westward Ho! and North Devon Ladies' Golf Clubs formed four years later.

1865 (Royal) Liverpool Golf Club formed at Hoylake some 15 miles from the city.

1866 4000 golfers now worldwide. 99% in Britain at 38 clubs over 24 courses. The number of clubs was to double by 1876.

1867 Report that a ladies' 'short course' had been laid out at St Andrews, a ladies' club was also set up. A subsequent report says the short course was ill-kept and 'barely fit for rabbits'.

1871 (Royal) Adelaide Golf Club formed. The first in Australia. Club revived 20 years later. Otago Golf Club became first in New Zealand.

1872 London Scottish Ladies Golf Club formed at Wimbledon. It ceased to function in 1879 but was revived in 1890.

1873 (Royal) Montreal Golf Club formed. The first in Americas.

1878 First golf club in South America at Buenos Aires.

1881 (Royal) Belfast Golf Club formed. First in Ireland.

1885 (Royal) Cape Golf Club formed in South Africa.

1888 First courses in USA (the St Andrews club in Yonkers). Club set aside $28.00 for annual course maintenance.
First course in Wales (Tenby).

2 Starting from Scratch

Jessica Issette Frances Pearson was born on November 2nd, 1862, at the family's holiday home of Soldier's Point on the North Wales island of Anglesey. The Pearson family were famous publishers in London where Issette grew up, playing her golf at Wimbledon from 1886. At that time Issette was the only female member of the club, but following the split from the military club, and aided by the renewal of interest amongst other ladies, Issette was instrumental in reforming the Wimbledon Ladies' Club in 1890. The first secretary was, appropriately, Miss Tee.

Issette found a firm friend and adviser in Dr William Laidlaw-Purves, a London eye-surgeon who had played a large part in the separation of the two clubs. Originally Purves was from Edinburgh and he told Issette that many women played golf in Scotland. It was still believed, a century later, that there were no women golfers anywhere in the world at that time.

Purves was a dynamic but abrasive character who had been trying to organise men's golf in Britain since the 1880s. The problem with men's golf was simple: everyone accepted that there had to be a central controlling body – but nobody was trusted enough to allow any progress to be made. Purves tried to galvanise interest without success, until eventually he wearied of being 'a prophet without honour' and devoted his time to his three obsessions – his own golf, supporting Issette and playing his part in the growth of the sport.

Issette Pearson (circa 1900)

The sudden increase in building golf courses at the end of the 19th century owed much to an unlikely source: the great railway companies were all in fierce competition and they had to be constantly producing new sporting events to put bottoms on railway seats. Some railway companies organised boxing matches, whilst others looked to a group of entrepreneurs led by Purves to produce income from the new sport of golf.

Purves was quick to recognise the potential for 'links' golf courses on the South East coast. He would travel to the end of a railway line and look at adjacent land that was too poor for farming, and could be obtained cheaply. He would buy the land, open a golf course and the railway would provide the customers.

Subsequent biographers have attributed to Purves the title of 'golf architect' which is slightly incorrect. Purves always paid a golf professional to design the 18 holes.

The doctor was an incredibly prolific creator of new golf courses (notably Littlestone and Royal St George's) but he was no diplomat and invariably ended up falling out with his collaborators.

It is strange that Purves and Issette managed to get on so well together, because they were both high-handed autocrats with a great gift for upsetting people.

Under Purves' advice and Issette's captaincy, Wimbledon Ladies began playing matches with other ladies' clubs. This included making the long railway journey to Minchinhampton in Gloucestershire. In the top match, Issette played and lost to Minchinhampton's No. 1 player, Lady Margaret Scott. This was a result that was to be repeated before long at the highest level.

These matches encouraged Issette to form a 'ladies union' – to encourage the female game and to create an organisation that would avoid the problems that were besetting the men's game. She wrote to dozens of clubs with lady members, and asked them to send representatives to a meeting on 19th April, 1893, at the Grand Hotel, London. Sixty-three clubs sent representatives and on that day, the meeting formed the Ladies Golf Union, appointing Miss Pearson as Honorary Secretary. Issette used her home address of 10 Northumberland Avenue, Putney as the LGU's offices and gave the LGU its telegraph address of 'ISSETTE'.

During the Grand Hotel meeting, the new course at St Anne's in Lancashire offered their forthcoming 'Open Ladies' meeting as the first Championship for the new association. The meeting accepted the offer because the Lancashire club had an unequalled reputation of treating its female members with fairness, and this could not be said of many of the older and more famous courses. The competition ran from June 13th – 18th, 1893, and although 38 ladies from the cream of English society competed, the local newspaper reported only that with so many attractive young females about 'a young man might do his courting on the putting green in preference to the drawing room'.

THE FIRST GREAT STYLIST

In 1893, St Anne's golf course was one mile north of the present royal championship course. It was short but tricky, which the experts thought would suit the local hopefuls. The greater experience of the southern girls soon became apparent as Issette Pearson reached the final. She was joined by the Earl of Eldon's beautiful dark-haired daughter Lady Margaret Scott (1875 – 1938), who became the first great female golfer. Her success was so phenomenal she was eulogised for decades afterwards, and biographers lavished outlandish claims upon her, including crediting her with being the first lady to flight a golf ball. This claim ignores the fact that some Scottish lady golfers of the time were hitting the ball nearly 150 yards, which is virtually impossible to do along the ground.

Certainly, her ladyship was the first great stylist in ladies' golf, with a long

exaggerated swing she had learnt from her three brothers Denys, Michael and Osmund who were all top-class amateurs. Osmund was runner-up in the 1905 Amateur Championship and Michael won four Australian titles and the (British) Amateur championship at the age of 55.

St Anne's, Lancashire. The competitors in the first ever LGU Championship

The family had recreated the ancient Scots tradition of the very rich by building their own golf course on the family estate at Stowell Park in Gloucestershire. With five golfers in the family, the Eldons were able to play the premier local clubs on equal terms with Margaret as the only female player on either side.

Lady Margaret had little difficulty disposing of Issette in the first LGU final. Although the Wimbledon girl was an accomplished iron player, she was a poor putter and suffered badly from pre-match nerves. Lady Margaret on the other hand never allowed anything to upset her. Lady Margaret Scott was superior to any other girl player of her time and retired undefeated after a hat-trick of LGU wins at Lytham, Littlestone in 1894 and Portrush in 1895. Whilst she never played a competitive round in Britain after 1895, she won three Swiss ladies' titles from 1907 to 1909 under her married name of Lady Hamilton-Russell.

The great golf writer Bernard Darwin said Lady Scott was the best woman player he ever saw. However, modern opinion is that she was a large fish in a very small pool – but the pool was growing larger every year.

THE ORR SISTERS' BRIEF DIP IN THE POOL

When Issette first met Dr Laidlaw-Purves she was surprised by his assertion that there were many talented lady golfers in Scotland. If they existed, they

were apathetic to the English-organised British Championship.

During Lady Margaret Scott's hat-trick of LGU wins, the Scots had never shown any interest in competing and the following year at Royal Liverpool, they were noticeable again by their absence. Two Wimbledon girls Amy Pascoe and Lena Thomson fought out the final, Miss Pascoe emerging as victor.

Issette's answer was 'if the mountain won't come to the prophet', it was time for the prophet to visit East Lothian. So in 1897, the LGU took the competition to the historic links of Gullane near the resort of North Ber-

1897 LGU Championship, Gullane. Issette Pearson with the starters

wick, known in the 1890s as 'the Biarritz of the North'.

North Berwick was a town built on golf. The great Scots professional Ben Sayers was its most famous resident. The municipality had a short ladies' nine-hole course, but allowed the best lady golfers to play over the men's 18-hole course. The three daughters of a Turkish carpet importer were the best local players, but were total unknowns to Issette and the other competitors. By the middle of the week Edith, Emily and Aimee Orr were national celebrities.

One hundred and five entrants started the competition, 55 from England

and Wales, ten from Ireland and 40 from Scotland. The visitors were crushed as thirteen of the last sixteen were unknown Scots.

The 1897 final is still remembered in North Berwick, with Miss Edith Orr against Miss Aimee Orr. A crowd estimated at 2,000 gathered as a large percentage of North Berwick's population journeyed five miles down the coast. Gullane's public houses did unprecedented business on the final day and caddies gambled £5 notes on the result, before Edith beat Aimee 4 and 2.

The Orr Family were strict Presbyterian and the gambling and drunkenness of the crowd horrified the sisters' father. He instantly forbade their participation in any competitive golf. The girls accepted their father's stricture without objection and returned home to a life of local uncompetitive golf and Sunday school teaching. Even after their father's death 20 years later, none of the sisters ever entered another championship, took a job or married. The tall and strongly built Orr sisters were a regular sight in North Berwick until their deaths in the 1950s.

Golf had lost three great players to the Church of Scotland, but it was obvious that Scottish ladies' golf was flourishing long before Issette Pearson organised her meeting at the Grand. Her golfing reputation had also suffered by her own disappointing performances in the LGU's major championship. She was becoming increasingly aware that what had been championship standard in 1893 was some way below the level of the new wave of talented young girls emerging from Scotland, Northern England and particularly from Ireland.

IRISH GIRLS TO THE FORE

As part of Issette's missionary work to encourage ladies' golf (and membership of the LGU), she took the championship to every part of Britain. She began with the Northern Ireland course of Portrush in 1895. The youngest competitor at Portrush was 13-year-old May Hezlet, who scored a disastrous 110 in the medal round.

This dismal performance spurred May to work harder at her game. She soon began to rival another Ulster girl, Rhoda Adair, as local champion; indeed the two youngsters soon became a match for any lady player in the region.

In 1899, the chance came for May to avenge her failure of four years before, when the LGU Championship visited the beautiful course of Royal County Down (where the Mountains of Mourne really do roll down to the sea). Her victory in the final a week after her 17th birthday was doubly sweet for she laid the ghost of 1894. The previous week she had won the Irish Ladies' title. She remains the youngest winner of the British Championip.

If local knowledge could be used as an excuse for the Irish win in 1899, then no such reason could be given the following year for another Irish win by Rhoda Adair at Westward Ho! Contemporary accounts blamed the state of the course for the high scoring, but perhaps the LGU were struggling to explain another disappointing championship for the English contingent. It

1897 LGU Championship, Gullane. The two Orr sisters – Edith (left) and Aimee (right) – with the trophy

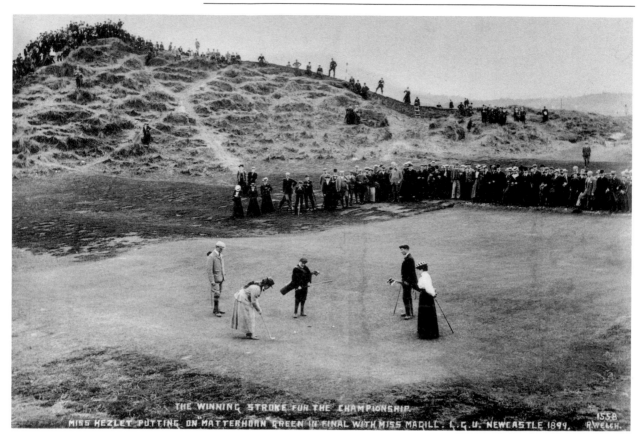

THE WINNING STROKE FOR THE CHAMPIONSHIP.
MISS HEZLET PUTTING ON MATTERHORN GREEN IN FINAL WITH MISS MAGILL. L.G.U. NEWCASTLE 1899.

May Hezlet sinks the winning putt in the 1899 LGU Championship, Royal County Down

was the Irish and Scots girls who stole the Westward Ho! show.

Molly and Sybil Whigham, two girls from Prestwick, had spectators gasping as they consistently drove the ball 200 yards and more. From the 18th tee, Molly managed a drive of 234 yards. This made a joke of Lord Westwood's famous 1892 statement that 'women were physically incapable of hitting a golf ball any further than 70 yards'. Despite their awesome power, the Whigham girls did not have the short game to compete with Rhoda Adair who beat Edith Nevile in the final.

May Hezlet won three British titles and Rhoda two before marriage brought about early retirement.

HOYLAKE GIRLS

The year 1901 brought much relief at LGU Headquarters, as the domination of the Irish and Scots girls was broken by Molly Graham from Moreton Ladies' Golf Club in Cheshire. Rather like buses, champions from Moreton came in twos, and she was quickly followed by Lottie Dod from the same club.

The tall, strongly built Molly Graham (1880 – 1955) was the sister of two of Royal Liverpool's greatest players, John and Allan Graham. Molly learnt her golf from her father at Royal Liverpool despite the club's ban on ladies.

This lasted until 1957 when the Royal Liverpool Ladies' Golf Club was formed. This exclusion was not taken too seriously because generations of club officials had turned a blind eye to women's presence on the course and the ladies found a home at the nearby Moreton Ladies' Golf Club.

In a short but spectacular golfing career, Molly took the 1901 British title and the second Scottish Ladies' title in 1904. Her win in the 1901 British Championship at Aberdovey is best remembered for an incident in her semi-final. This was against Mrs Stubbs, whose score at the 8th hole was wrongly recorded as a 7 to halve the hole; it had actually been an 8. Spectators murmured their protest, but Molly Graham accepted her opponent's score without question. The disputed hole gave Mrs Stubbs a one stroke win and therefore entry into the final.

Molly was prevailed upon to protest about the incident at the 8th hole and Competition Secretary, Issette Pearson, decreed a play-off which Molly won. This paved the way to a 3 and 1 win in the final against Rhoda Adair.

Despite this meteoric success, Molly failed to win another British title and lost interest in golf altogether. Between the wars she began playing again and on one occasion beat her nephew John Graham, who was a Walker Cup trialist, 9 an 8. John was 19 and Molly was over 60!

Molly's family are one of Liverpool's great sporting dynasties, but their achievements are dwarfed by the prodigious Dod family of nearby Bebington who excelled at every sport Victorian life had to offer. Their four children were all champions, but only one youngster is remembered today: the peerless Lottie Dod.

Charlotte Dod (1871 – 1960) packed more into her life than most people. She began by winning the Wimbledon Ladies' Tennis Championship at 16 years of age. She held the title for six years, mainly because the champion was only challenged once a year by the winner of the preliminary rounds (who was usually on the verge of exhaustion). To be fair to Lottie, she lost only half a dozen games of tennis in ten years, so she must have been a fine champion. Eventually, being Wimbledon tennis champion can become rather tedious, so Lottie tried hockey (and won an international cap), and then turned to mountaineering before golf took her interest.

Lottie reached the semi-finals of the British Championships in 1898 and became England's premier player in the Home Internationals but this caused friction with Issette Pearson. Playing in the Home Internationals for three days before the LGU Championships put considerable pressure on international players. The situation was worse for Lottie as she suffered from a bad back. Understandably she felt that 36 holes of golf every day for a week for someone with sciatica was too much; Issette dismissed her protestations. Eventually Lottie made the British Ladies' Finals in 1904 at Troon where she had to face May Hezlet in the final. There was a crowd of 3,000 spectators. Lottie established an early one hole lead and although Miss Hezlet fought strongly Lottie won at the 18th. The win made Lottie the only girl to be British tennis and golf champion.

In 1904 Lottie was invited by the USGA to play in the US Women's

Rhoda Adair – generally held to be the world's best lady golfer in 1900

1904 LGU Championship at Troon. Lottie Dod putts

Championship, even though they had to change their own rules to allow her admission. Due to lack of practice, Lottie was eliminated in the first round. However, during the visit she arranged a match between the American Ladies visiting Britain the following summer and a British team. This eventually led to the Curtis Cup.

The trip gives some insight into Lottie's phenomenal ability as a tennis player for 1908 US Tennis Doubles champion and four times US golf champion Margaret Curtis invited Lottie to play a game of tennis. Poor Miss Curtis lost 6-1, 6-0.

On her return to England, Lottie announced her retirement from golf. She compensated by taking up archery, and she subsquently represented Great Britain in the 1908 Olympics. After the First World War, Lottie regained her zest for golf at Westward Ho! and also became President of Devon Ladies. She died in 1960, and legend has it that she slipped away whilst listening to the Wimbledon tennis championship on the radio.

By the time of her death, Lottie would have hardly recognised the sports of tennis and golf which she had played with such distinction in a different age. But what Lottie and other British champions had done was to spread the word throughout the world that ladies' golf could be a vibrant and well-organised game. In countries such as America, the authorities were becoming convinced that Issette Pearson and her LGU may well have created the ideal framework for men's and women's golf.

3 The Czar of Golf

I n a few short years around the turn of the century, ladies' golf became a popular pastime all over the world and if imitation was the sincerest form of flattery, then the LGU had much to be proud of. Emerging counties were copying the LGU framework, and many were affiliating to the British body. They recognised that the way the LGU was organised meant that there was a place for every player from the humblest hacker, to the Lottie Dods of this world.

Like all successful developments, the LGU framework was not a lucky accident. It was a deliberate plan with Issette Pearson as architect. Some commentators were not so flattering about the 'Hon Sec', preferring to call her the Czar of Golf.

Despite her earlier championship form, at 40 Issette had to accept that she just could not beat every new girl who came into the game. Plus, she had plenty of work off the course with LGU membership rising to 20,000 before falling back.

The success of the LGU was creating problems of its own. The philosopher who said ' Money isn't everything, but it's a long way in front of whatever's second' comprehensively described the LGU's greatest worry and obsession. But there was another major problem to overcome. Every club affiliated to the LGU had different criteria for assessing playing ability. They tried to follow the Royal and Ancient's rules on competition, but the rules were vague and had been written in an era when there were only 4,000 golfers in the world (99% of whom wore a kilt and sporran).

When a ladies' open meeting was held, the clubs firstly tried to give every player an equal opportunity to win and secondly gave the officials a large bottle of aspirins. Players from small and easy courses would produce documents from their home club to say that they could get round 18 holes in 80 strokes; top-class players who played over men's courses would have documents that said they could play 18 holes in 95. Obviously the top class players were not 15 strokes worse than the girls from smaller clubs, so competition secretaries would try to award handicaps on the day of the meeting. With 100 or more competitors, the result was usually unbridled chaos.

A radical solution was needed urgently if the ladies' game was not to deteriorate into the sad state of men's British amateur golf. Ladies' golf had been

Tommy Miller with the two Mrs Millers. Left to right: Belle Miller, Issette Pearson, Tommy Miller Jnr

created by Issette under the golf umbrella of the LGU, therefore there was scope for a grand solution. Also, Issette Pearson was a pragmatist who had the power to introduce change to the ladies' game without great opposition. The vast majority of LGU members were girls who wanted to play golf with the minimum of off-course effort on their part. If some woman in Wimbledon wanted to spend her life worrying about the administration of the game, then good for her.

In August, 1895, Issette began trials with a variation of Purves' handicapping system. Basically, women golfers would come into three categories – Bronze, Silver and Gold. These represented ability, from new players (who would receive 36 strokes) up to the best (scratch) players. This system was supported by the need to lodge complete scorecards with the club officials and the appointment of regional experts called 'handicap advisers'. Top class

Issette (now Mrs Miller) in 1913

players toured the country and played several (free) rounds at each affiliated course to assess the SSS, Standard Scratch Score.

According to Elsie Corlett (1901–1988), who was a great friend of Issette's, the proposals for 'handicapping players' were viewed as hilarious by the British men's golfing authorities, but they were soon laughing on the other side of their faces when the United States Golf Association adopted their own version for both American ladies' and mens' golf. Eventually, in the 1920s, the strength of American opinion forced the British men to re-consider their rejection of Issette's and Purves' ideas.

Issette herself wrote that the term 'handicapping' came from horse-racing, where all the horses in a particular race receive weight from the best horse and in theory should have an equal chance. She added that the actual handicap, was based on an ancient form of bartering by farmers at markets. Each bidder put his money and hand into a cap to conceal the size of the bid from the opposition. When all the bidders had put their money and hands into the cap, an arbiter opened the cap and counted the offers.

If Issette was obsessed with fairness on the golf course, she sometimes fell below that aim in her own dealings with other people. The title of 'the Czar' was bestowed on her by the enraged press when she banned them from covering an LGU final because she felt they were upsetting the players. They never forgave her. She could not see their point of view and a trivial issue became a major public row – a process that was repeated soon afterwards, with potentially more serious results, over the matter of paying expenses for county matches.

Following the successful introduction of handicapping, fair competition became a reality and county organisations were formed to help organise the sport. But in contrast to the well-heeled girls with private incomes that Issette mixed with, some of the county players were from relatively modest backgrounds and they needed help with their travelling expenses.

Issette was totally opposed to paying expenses, but she was stymied when the campaign found a champion in her Wimbledon teammate, Eveline Phillips. The issue rumbled on for years until matters reached a crisis point. A golfing magazine carried an attack on Issette's stand against expenses and amongst the magazine's contributors was Issette's assistant Mabel Stringer. 'Auntie Mabel', as everyone knew her, was not the flavour of the month around Northumberland Avenue, Putney, for some time afterwards.

Issette was determined to rid the LGU of Miss Phillips, whom she blamed for the article. This was achieved by accusing her former friend of fiddling LGU expenses. The ill-feeling engendered by the sacking led to the creation of a breakaway organisation called the 'National Alliance'. They tried to oust Issette and to set up an English version of the LGU (Scotland, Wales and Ireland already had their own unions). The Alliance organised two English Championships before the First World War ended their interest in golf.

The Hon Sec may have made a dreadful mess of her dealings with the press and many of her own members, but on occasions she could display great skill in handling opponents. Never more so than in thwarting Mrs Pankhurst's suffragettes, who had many supporters amongst lady golfers. In 1912 the King's horse was brought down during the Derby by a suffragette running on to the track. A year later, Princess Victoria's visit to the LGU championship at Lytham brought threats of vandalism. But the suffragettes had not reckoned with Issette. She hired boy scouts to police the course and afterwards, each scout troop was presented with an engraved staff.

The threat to the LGU had been averted at very little financial cost by Issette's unusual style of man (or woman) management. She had made mistakes but she always managed to ensure that the sport of ladies' golf came out on top. Perhaps the LGU's survival was Issette's greatest achievement, but many good judges consider that nothing equalled her skilful handling of Cecil Leitch, who became the sport's first great star and who sparked the incredible boom that ladies' golf enjoyed between the wars.

4 Cecil Leitch

All great sporting fiction centres on the unknown outsider who turns up at the big event and takes the world by storm. In women's golf, this actually happened. In 1908, a young lass from Silloth, a small, picturesque seaside town twenty miles west of Carlisle, arrived at St Andrews for the British Ladies' Open Championship. Upsetting greater names, she drove her way into the semi-finals where she was stopped, not by the eventual winner, but by her only wood, which split while she was in a commanding lead.

This unknown player was Charlotte Cecilia Pitcairn Leitch (1891 – 1977). Known simply as 'Cecil', she was one of five daughters (Edith, May, Cecilia, Chris and Peggy) and two sons (Moncrieff and William) born to a Fife doctor who practised in Silloth, and who founded the first golf course there, near the site of the present 18-hole championship course.

NEW GIRLS FROM NOWHERE

Silloth teenagers tended to remain in Silloth, remote and isolated. Since there was little fun to be had in this charming backwater, the Leitch children were taught to play golf by their father, and they played endless games together. They battled with old clubs against the thick heather and stiff westerly winds, and they became very proficient. In 1908, a woman visitor from Yorkshire, cast a weather eye over them and persuaded the family to let Cecil and sister Edith travel to St Andrews for the British Ladies' Open. The family would have probably refused, but as the Leitches had relatives in St Andrews, this seems to have swayed the balance.

Issette Pearson was amazed at the precocious talent of these two young girls. Silloth, after all, didn't even have a county team. In the Championship, Edith, aged 19, beat three vastly more experienced women and Cecil carried all before her until her wood let her down. She lost in the semi-final to the eventual champion, Miss Maud Titterton, a player with more than a decade of top-class experience. But the crowd and the newspapers took the new girls to their hearts. Issette earmarked Cecil and her big sister Edith as top class players, a position they were rapidly to achieve.

Edith Leitch, now 20, made her international debut in the 1909 Home International series and was an England International for twenty years. Un-

fortunately, Cecil was not eligible for England. The LGU rules at that time stated that a player had either to have English parentage, or to have lived in England for twenty years. Cecil had a Scots father, and she was only 18. This meant that she did not qualify for any country.

Miss Pearson decided to alter the rulebook to cater for Cecil and for any other talented youngster who might find herself in limbo. Sister May also made the England team in 1912. Cecil considered May to be the finest left-hander of her era. Their two sisters, Chris and Peg, were good enough to compete in the 1912, 1913 and 1914 Ladies' Opens. But this was not the end of the Leitch family's talent. Reputedly the best of all the seven youngsters was Moncrieff, or 'Moni' as they called him, but he never had the chance to shine. He died of consumption in 1907, at the age of 22.

Edith and Cecil were interested, if rain-sodden, spectators at the 1908 final. This was wrecked by a storm which damaged the LGU's property, including an expensive new flag donated by Miss Pearson's future husband, Lancashire textile millionaire Tommy Miller. Such donations kept the LGU afloat. To save money, the Home International championship was staged the week before the British Ladies' Open. Indeed, the lack of cash meant that only two major titles were available to women players – the Ladies' Open and the National Closed Championship (the English version of which was founded in 1912). Curiously in subsequent years, 'Closed' became 'Close'.

After 1908, Cecil completed in the Ladies' Open but, despite her growing reputation as the Golden Girl of British Sport, she never progressed beyond the semi-finals. Nevertheless, Issette Pearson, had no qualms about ranking her England Number One, nor about her becoming the first player in history to be granted a plus 1 handicap. Miss Pearson had introduced handicapping and would do as she thought fit with it.

MATCHED AGAINST MEN

Issette did acknowledge a major problem with Cecil Leitch: she could never produce her best form at match-play. The 'Hon Sec' thought that Cecil was the victim of her own success. Isolated out on the Cumberland coast and without a county association to represent, Cecil had competed mainly in local competitions against her own family and friends. In 1909 she posted Silloth's course record of 72, playing off the men's tees – one of the rare examples of a woman holding a full course record.

Issette's solution was somewhat radical. She recommended that Cecil should compete against the top men at match-play. And as even the unusually gifted Cecil Leitch couldn't hope to match the top men in distance from the tee, she was allowed 9 strokes per 18 holes. The result was, that over the next two years, Miss Leitch enhanced her national standing by holding her own in public matches against some of the greatest names in men's golfing history.

She took on five-times Open Champion James Braid at his own club,

OPPOSITE ABOVE Silloth-on-Solway GC holding a competition in August 1907

LEFT Cecil Leitch (centre) with brother Moncrieff (left) and the Silloth professional, 1907

FAR LEFT The new wondergirl of British golf, Cecil Leitch, photographed during early rounds at St Andrews, 1908

Walton Heath. Braid was the greatest match-play golfer of his era and was at his peak when they met. Huge crowds turned out to watch the encounter, as they did at Royal Liverpool for her meeting with 1909 PGA Match-play Champion, Tom Ball.

Public interest in these early 'Battles of the Sexes' reached fever pitch in 1909, when Cecil faced Harold Hilton over 72 holes. Winner of the Open and Amateur titles, Hilton was a golfing legend in the years before the First World War, not least because he had crossed the Atlantic and snatched away the US Amateur title in 1911, becoming the first Briton to hold both national amateur titles at the same time. Now, at Walton Heath and in front of over 3,000 people, Hilton was beaten by a girl.

Cecil's match-play improved enough for her to win the 1912 French Open, but the British Ladies' title continued to elude her. Eventually, in 1914, she opted to move to London and play for Hertfordshire and the Bushey Hall Club. She had decided to lick her match-play into shape, and now she reaped the rewards, by landing the big double. She won the British Ladies' Open at Hunstanton, and the new English Close Championship.

It was inevitable that Cecil would move to the South. It was not for the bright lights and glamour of the big city, but to be closer to the expensive new London courses that were organizing top-class competitions for women. The girl from Silloth was now a major celebrity, fascinating to the public whether they cared about golf or not. Ever since she had stolen the headlines at St Andrews, Cecil had been a national figure with 'style' and 'charisma'. She attracted attention because she was the first girl who dressed to play golf rather than wearing the prim Victorian style of her predecessors. Her clothes were those of a woman golfer trying to hit the ball much further than any woman had done before.

THE LEITCH SWING

The great Cumbrian Men's champion Alf Greave, who was twenty years her junior, recalled in 1926 seeing Cecil play from the first tee at Silloth. He vividly remembers that, despite a breeze in her face, she was capable of reaching the 'horseshoe', a hummock 220 yards up the fairway – something few men could achieve. A description of her swing, from around the same time, describes her stance as being wider than usual and commented that she put every ounce of her considerable upper-body strength into dispatching the ball. For most people, this all or nothing style leads to the ball and club-face being out of alignment on impact, usually with disastrous results. For Cecil it worked superbly.

The 'War to End All Wars' now began. After 1916, golf like many sports, fell into decline as the appalling war casualties took their toll on Britain's men. Women quietly filled their jobs. Cecil devoted herself to voluntary work in London and Carlisle for four years. It was a period of reappraisal for the role of women in society, and within a short time they had fought for, and won, the vote.

RIGHT 1914 British Championship. After six years of failure, Cecil Leitch finally wins the big event at Hunstanton

In 1919, for those lucky enough to be in one piece, golf resumed. Cecil's sister May had qualified as an orthopaedist and she gave up the game to concentrate on her medical career. Edith and Cecil, however, were still the backbone of the England team. The 1919 British Ladies' Open had to be postponed. The existing handicaps were years out of date, there weren't enough players, and there was also a rail strike. But the English Close Championship was held at St Anne's Old Links – the venue for the first British Ladies' Open in 1893 – and here Cecil simply carried on where she had left off. She notched up two more British Opens when these resumed, giving her a hat-trick spread over eight years: 1914, 1920 and 1921.

WEATHERING WETHERED

The 1920 English Championship, however, brought a shock for Miss Leitch. For the first time, her indomitable style faced a serious challenge from a newcomer, and she was forced into second place. The newcomer was Joyce Wethered, the sister of Britain's top amateur, Roger Wethered. She had learnt the game from her brother, and she meant business. Her dramatic victory in the English Championship – her debut in top-class competition – was particularly bewildering to the LGU because she had no handicap. All they could do in the circumstances was to assess her as plus 1 – the first recorded case of a golfer going straight on to a plus handicap (Cecil's had taken longer).

Miss Wethered was a totally different player to Miss Leitch. Whereas the Silloth girl had achieved her powerhouse game by mastering inclement weather and conditions, and technical deficiencies, this newcomer was a genius. Where Cecil had to overcome nature, Miss Wethered had nature on her side. She possessed an innate gift for golf, and no less a player than Bobby Jones thought she was the finest striker of a golf ball he ever saw – male or female.

Cecil Leitch, like the champion she was, avenged herself the following year in the finals of the British Ladies' and French Opens. But Miss Wethered held on to the English title. From 1920 to 1926, the British public were captivated by these two arch-rivals. Their battles were heroic, yet romantic.

Their personalities were poles apart. Cecil was a no-nonsense Northern girl who enjoyed the fame and attention that her hard work had brought her. Joyce Wethered was brilliant at golf, but painfully shy. Cecil had an entrepreneurial spirit, marching on St Andrews and London from her little town in Cumberland to take the golfing world by storm. Miss Wethered came from polite society and a wealthy London family. Whenever the two girls met, each had in tow charabancs of devoted followers – even though fans were unusual at this time.

Who was the greater golfer? English champion and contemporary Elsie Corlett always maintained that Cecil Leitch was the better player. She felt that if the Kaiser hadn't intervened, Miss Leitch would certainly have won eight straight Opens instead of the four she ended up with.

In October 1921, Cecil and her sister Edith were invited to America and Canada to take part in their Open championships. Their trip was a mixture of tragedy and high romance. Short of practice, neither girl gave her best in the US Open, but in the Canadian championship, Cecil rewrote the record books. In the semi-final, Edith had lost to a local girl, Mollie McBride. Rumour has it that this had been a needle match. Cecil went out on to the course for the 36-hole final with Miss McBride in no mood to take prisoners.

By lunchtime, the unfortunate Miss McBride was 14 down. Cecil maintains that the young woman insisted on continuing, although some observers thought she wanted to stay in the clubhouse, and that Cecil had forced her out. The organisers tried to cancel the second round to spare embarrassment, but they did not succeed. On the course, the Canadian girl immediately lost the first three holes, and the record shows that C Leitch beat M McBride 17 up with 15 to play – the biggest hiding in a major event in the history of golf. Cecil said that she had humiliated her opponent because she was a poor golfer who should never have been in the final.

Whatever the reason, shortly afterwards Cecil injured her arm. The accident was sufficiently serious to send her home to England, where a doctor forbade her to play golf for two years. Six months later, defiant as ever, Cecil

1920 English Championship, Sherringham. Cecil Leitch completes her card, unaware that a new girl, Joyce Wethered, was to prove the champion

37

A portrait of Cecil Leitch by Cecil Beaton, 1926

entered the British Open. She reached the final where she was crushed by Joyce Wethered 9 and 7. The defeat had a salutory effect, and Miss Leitch put away her clubs. She did not play again for eighteen months.

THE TWILIGHT YEARS

Her old adversary now took a stranglehold on the women's game, and it culminated in Joyce winning the British and English titles in 1924. Cecil, who by then had recovered from her injury, won the French Open at Le Touquet. She and Edith were still members of the England team, and they had something else to celebrate in Edith's marriage to the brother of Phillip Guardella, the philosopher.

From the golfing point of view, the best was yet to come, and 1925 was to see the greatest final ever played out in the British Ladies' Open. Leitch and Wethered fought out 36 holes at Troon, forcing the best out of each other and forcing superlatives out of even the most hardened golf journalists. Level after 36 holes, it was Miss Wethered who finally took the 37th hole, and with it the title and trophy, all amid a bedlam of cheers. Cecil made no excuses. She said that in her whole career, she had never played so well as in this defeat – the supreme compliment to her opponent.

Now in her late thirties and with many other outside interests, Cecil decided to semi-retire from competitive golf. But there was life in the old tigress yet. In 1926, she decided she would try for a unique quartet of British Open titles. She had won in England in 1914 (at Hunstanton), in Ireland in 1920 (at Newcastle), and in Scotland in 1921 (at Turnberry). Now, at Royal St Davids in Wales, she produced a fitting swan song, beating Mrs Garon of Essex by 8 and 7 to round off her British tour de force. In celebration, the newly founded BBC interviewed her about her victory on the new wireless.

Everything about Cecil's career is larger than life, and the end was no exception. Invited back to the scene of her former triumph for the 1927 British Open at Newcastle, County Down, the great Cecil Leitch was struck by lightning. She took no further part in the competition and, although she carried on playing golf socially for the rest of her life, this was the end of her competitive career in the game. She became a businesswoman, first in antiques and later in entertainment.

In 1927, she resigned from her post as council member of the LGU, over the continuing matter of paying expenses. Her relations with the LGU had been less than cosy since they had investigated her own and Joyce Wethered's successful forays into golf book writing. Cecil's attitude to earning money from golf seems slightly ambiguous.

Cecil's sister, Edith, won the 1928 English title. She was killed in 1942, whilst on active service with the WRAC, and Cecil herself died in 1978, at the age of 86. In later years, she received a small part of the serious recognition that her golfing exploits merited. Colgate opened a museum to house a golf collection that she and the Veteran Ladies' Golf Association had assembled before the war, but this eventually was passed to the Golf Museum at St Andrews.

Cecil was a tireless worker for the Veteran Ladies' GA, and a vice-president of the National Playing Fields Association. The LGU, their feathers ruffled by Cecil over the years, nevertheless recognised her importance. She wielded much influence and eventually persuaded them to award Silloth-on-Solway Golf Club the 1972 and 1976 English and British Ladies' championships. Cecil attended both. Her visit in 1972 was her first return home since her mother had died in 1937.

Miss Leitch has always been revered in America as the first great woman golfer, and American tourists arriving in Silloth are always astonished to find that there is no museum to her memory. In Britain she is remembered only by a handful of friends and acquaintances. The British golfing establishment, long after South African apartheid reforms in sport, still allows women to be banned from courses and clubhouses in its domain. It clearly considers that women golfers should be seen and not heard of. Let us hope that, in years to come, it pays due tribute to Cecil Leitch.

5 'The Greatest'

It is difficult for modern golf fans to grasp the hero-worship that 1920s golfing supporters showered upon Cecil Leitch and her arch-rival Joyce Wethered. Nobody was neutral. Everybody had an opinion on who was 'the greatest'. Bobby Jones never had any doubts. He said Joyce was the best golfer, man or woman, he had seen, and there could be no greater accolade.

Miss Wethered was born on 17th November, 1901, at Malden in Surrey. Her father was a talented painter from Yorkshire but her brother Roger was a master with the golf club. He was captain of Oxford and only lost the 1922 Open Championship after a play-off.

Joyce was slow to develop as a golfer, until Roger persuaded her to abandon her natural flat swing and to develop a more upright style. This dramatic change in her style took her to the last four of the 1920 Surrey Ladies' Championship on her competition debut. Surrey Ladies were impressed, but not too impressed. They put her at the bottom of order of play for the county team.

LUCK AND TALENT

After this modest debut, Joyce entered the 1920 English Close Championship at Sheringham. She reached the final where she came up against the World's Number One player, Cecil Leitch. Incredibly, the inexperienced girl won the match. As Miss Wethered collected the huge silver trophy she looked tired and drawn. She was suffering from whooping cough and it was to keep her indoors for the next three months.

In 1921, Cecil Leitch had her revenge in the final of the British Championship. Joyce had a terrible morning and was trailing by 7 holes at lunch, but in the afternoon, she retaliated with an astonishing sequence of shots to produce a revival of Lazarus proportions before losing the Championship narrowly. Joyce regained her English title at Lytham winning 12 and 11, but this win was somewhat overshadowed by Cecil setting a world record 19 and 17 win in Canada.

The debate soon began about the merits of the two champions. Cecil had hurt her arm in America, and her doctor had prescribed rest, but Cecil felt the best cure would be a record fourth British title at Prince's, Sandwich. Sure enough the 1922 Final was what the fans wanted: Leitch v Wethered.

Two great champions – Simone de la Chaume of France (left) and Joyce Wethered of England (right)

For the match a gale blew off the Channel.

Joyce was determined not to give her opponent a seven strokes start this year, so she began like a whirlwind herself. Cecil would not fight back and it was soon obvious who the winner would be, as Cecil trailed the tall, thin youngster. An observer noted that the referee was a stocky Irish gentleman who was showing a total bias to Miss Leitch. After one brilliant shot from Miss Wethered, he threw his hat to the ground and told a bystander to take over. He reappeared long enough to announce that Joyce had won 9 and 7. The new champion smiled shyly and then confessed over dinner that she knew that she was going to win because she had found a 'lucky' black cat asleep on her bed at lunchtime.

THE GREATEST SHOCK IN LADIES' GOLF HISTORY

1923 began another year of triumph for Joyce when she recorded a hat-trick of English Championship wins at Ganton. *The Morning Post* said 'Miss Wethered is monotonously merciless with her opponents'. Whereas *The Leeds Mercury* said Joyce was the 'W G Grace of Golf'. They were obviously unaware that WG was famous for his bad temper on the golf course.

The year is best remembered however for one particular result. *The Daily Telegraph* predicted, that with Cecil Leitch still suffering with her arm injury, only Cheshire's Doris Chambers could hope to compete with the champion in the British Championship at lovely Burnham-on-Sea in Somerset. Everything went according to plan, until Joyce began what should have been a straight-forward semi-final against Mrs 'Doddy' Macbeth of Bowdon, (who as Muriel Dodd had won the title a decade before). Mrs Macbeth played superbly whereas Joyce was far below her best. The crowd and press could not believe their eyes when Mrs Macbeth won the match comfortably. The surprise proved too much for Doddy, and she lost the final to Doris Chambers by 2 holes.

But the defeat was soon forgotten as Joyce and top amateur Cyril Tolley set a new foursomes record at Worplesdon, winning an 18-hole match by 9 and 8 with only one hole halved. And purely for practice, Surrey and Middlesex played a friendly fixture at Northwood which brought Cecil Leitch and Joyce together for 18 holes with nothing at stake. Joyce won 5 and 3 but 1,000 spectators turned up and created chaos.

NOBODY'S DOORMAT

Joyce did not particularly enjoy the events at Northwood. The crowds loved her, but the youngster found it difficult to reciprocate and began to seriously consider retirement at the age of 22! But she continued playing and won both the English and British titles the following year.

In 1925, the British Championship at Troon was made far more interesting with the visit of the great American champion, Glenna Collett.

The new champion Joyce Wethered shows brilliant bunker play during the Worplesdon Mixed Foursomes

The world's richest man, John D Rockerfeller, had sponsored Glenna's visit and, on her departure for Scotland, he had presented her with a ten-cent piece as a good luck charm. 'That'll nae go far with Troon prices' was the comment at the Championship.

In the third round, the two girls met and were even at the ninth. Glenna topped her drive and fell away rapidly to finish 4 and 3 down.

Cecil Leitch awaited Joyce in the final and no woman's match in history has engendered so much interest. 8,000 spectators created havoc by blocking fairways and impeding the players. In a titanic match, Cecil got her nose in front at first, before Joyce grabbed a one shot lead near the end. But she quickly lost the advantage by missing the green at the 36th. As all was level, they played on and Joyce regained the lead at the 37th to take the match.

Miss Wethered was exhausted with the effort. She was also disillusioned with the crowd's ill-mannered behaviour. Even a rest from golf went wrong as she suffered a serious foot injury while playing tennis. She reappeared in the autumn and won the Worplesdon Foursomes with top amateur Edward Esmond, before announcing her retirement with the words, 'I have grown tired of being shoved around by crowds and I don't intend to be a doormat for that ill-mannered herd any longer'.

THE END OF AN ERA

For the next four years, Joyce resisted all overtures from those anxious to see her return to the centre of the golfing stage, but eventually in 1929 she agreed to come out of retirement to play in the British Championship at St Andrews. In a pre-tournament practice match, Miss Wethered played the famous Scots professional, Ted Blackwell. She beat him comfortably. It was said that even teetotallers drank strong liquor that night to recover from the shock of Blackwell's defeat.

In the Championship Final, Joyce defeated her old rival, Glenna Collett, in a match that she says gave her the greatest satisfaction of any win in her whole career, simply because her opponent played so magnificently.

The summer of 29 however marked the end of an era. The 'roaring twenties' gave way to the 'hungry thirties'. The great depression was looming and no one was spared. The Wall Street Crash of '29 swept away the Wethered family fortune and Joyce had to support herself.

She took a job as manageress of Fortnum and Mason's sports department. This was considered to be sailing rather close to the amateur wind. But she soon opted for professional status by playing in America. The trip guaranteed her £40 a round and netted over £10,000 in three months of matches with everybody who mattered in US golf. Bobby Jones, Walter Hagen, Gene Sarazen all helped make the tour a huge success.

American golf fans were anxious to compare the English girl with their new 'star', Babe Zaharias, who thought her opponent was under-powered. 'I can outdistance her driver with a two iron', said Babe, who omitted to mention that she had already lost two matches to the visitor.

'This was the most satisfying win of my career' – Joyce Wethered receives the British Championship trophy from the captain of St Andrews, 1929

On her return from the New World, Joyce married an old friend and Worplesdon regular Sir John Heathcoat-Amery of Knightshayes Court in Devon. Knightshayes Court is one of England's finest houses and the new Lady Amery set to work to bring the gardens up to the quality of the house. When the Second World War intervened, Lady Amery volunteered for a job in a factory inspecting aircraft parts. After the war Joyce and Sir John became occasional golfers and devoted their time to improving Knightshayes Court. Today Lady Amery still lives at Knightshayes Court and in 1988 opened a room displaying her golfing mementoes.

NEWS FROM THE HOME FRONT

As Lady Heathcoat-Amery worked on the wartime production line, news came through of another famous golfer at Singleton in Lancashire. Issette Pearson had died in her 80th year. Her funeral was a quiet affair. Rumour has it that most of the 'mourners' had only attended to make sure they had seen the last of the 'czar of golf'.

6 Twilight of the Czar

mid the success of Cecil Leitch and Joyce Wethered in the 1920s, the retirement of Issette Pearson as the LGU Secretary went almost unnoticed. Issette was now over sixty and her private circumstances had changed – but hardly for the worse.

Her marriage in 1912 to Tommy Miller Jnr of Singleton Park, Blackpool was short-lived as Tommy had died four years later.

Tommy, and his first wife Belle, had been close and supportive friends of Issette's since the LGU was created. Belle had helped as Assistant LGU Competition Secretary until her death in 1910. She was much loved in the hamlet of Singleton for her kind and considerate nature; a comment never made about her successor.

Tommy's father was a social climber, and had bought the squireship of Singleton one morning before breakfast without much knowledge of the locality. He was most unhappy therefore to discover that he was the squire of two rundown old farms and little else. He had then spent £400,000 building the village of Singleton, with the intention of building the perfect English Village. He could afford such luxury being the richest industrialist in the North West of England with 10,000 men, women and children working in his dark and dangerous mills for 20p a day.

Tommy Senior is forever remembered in English literature, because Charles Dickens portrayed him as the pennypinching Thomas Gradgrind in *Hard Times*, a novel about mill life.

Miller's first act as squire was to evict all Roman Catholics and also insist that the size of the village be kept below 360 to avoid building an almshouse for the poor. To supplement the resident estate staff, he hired casual labourers on a daily basis. They had to walk the two miles from the nearest town each day in the hope of a few shillings worth of work.

Tommy Junior was a much more pleasant person. He had a successful marriage to American girl Belle Byrne of New Orleans. In 1886 they became founder members of the Lytham and St Anne's Golf Club, and when the club hosted the first LGU Championship, the friendship between the Millers and Issette Pearson began.

The Millers at their majestic home at Singleton Hall, became willing hosts for large house parties involving all the top girl golfers and their gentlemen friends. Issette was a regular visitor. She and Tommy Junior had much in common, notably both being keen yacht sailors at the nearby Blackpool and Fleetwood Yacht Club.

On Tommy Junior's death in 1916 the estate passed not to Issette his widow, but to the only Miller son who was feeble minded. However, Issette took over the estate management and resigned as LGU Secretary.

As one of her first duties, she welcomed a new vicar, Thomas Hermon Watson, to the village. He was half Issette's age, but the two soon became close friends and lovers. The romance became the talk of the village where Issette rapidly lived up to her nickname of 'the czar'. She interfered in every aspect of village life from inspecting gardens for weeds to looking for children dropping litter.

Issette would use the village school as her personal labour exchange. If she needed gardeners, domestic staff or farm workers, she would arrive unannounced at the school and select the youngsters she wanted. They then had to pick up their belongings and would leave school for ever.

Her personal maid, Elsie Bailey (Southward), was recruited by this method and worked for Issette for 20 years. She remembers Issette as a cantankerous employer who sacked her once a month for years. It was up to Elsie to prepare the shopping list that was sent the 200 miles to Fortnum and Mason's in London. Issette would then dramatically reduce the list to a level that would have meant starvation rations for the entire household. Elsie used to 'adjust' the list back to a reasonable level and when the order was delivered she was invariably given the sack. Issette always relented but this pantomine was carried out every month for years.

Vicar Watson was a different sort of problem. As well as sharing Issette's bed, he persisted in getting village girls 'into trouble'. Issette grew so accustomed to this habit (he had seven illegitimate and eight legitimate children), that she made sure the unfortunates had somewhere to live. Local legend has it, that if the vicar had worn his trousers the same way that he wore his collar, Singleton would be half the size it is today.

Singleton village (circa 1925)

The last known photograph of Issette Pearson (Miller), on Coronation Day, 1937. Her close friend Vicar Watson is on her left

The vicar was married and despite this the two carried on their relationship. They even went away on Scottish fishing holidays together for many years.

Issette continued to play golf, as well as fishing, and was the pre-eminent member of Royal Lytham Ladies' Golf Club. The club's historian, Tony Nickson, managed to trace several members who had known Mrs Miller in the 1930s. One woman remembers an occasion when she was larking about on the first tee. A golf club servant arrived with a message ordering her to the ladies' lounge where Issette awaited her. She went back to the lounge full of dread, for she had heard of the stern Mrs Miller. Awaiting her was a tall, strongly built lady who quietly advised her that she should make better use of her time, if she wished to become a good player.

Issette played golf up until the week before her death on 25th April, 1941. It was a quiet funeral, conducted by Vicar Watson who died soon afterwards.

Her staff marked the death of 'the czar' by breaking out her best tea for a celebration cuppa. Elsie Bailey says 'We half expected her to rise up from her coffin and tell us to put it back.'

DIGGING UP THE PAST

Issette's home of Singleton Hall is today a home for handicapped children and out of school term is a quiet gloomy place where the lonely stranger treads warily, especially as the village is alive with ghost stories.

The churchyard is alleged to be haunted by one of Vicar Watson's predecessors and Singleton Hall is supposed to be haunted by a headless horse who gallops at night. The unfortunate animal is 'Honest Tom' who was Tommy Miller Jnr's pride and joy after winning first prize at the Royal Show. Tommy buried his favourite animal behind the Hall and erected a large headstone to its memory. Legend has it that the heartbroken Tom threw a handful of gold sovereigns into the grave as the horse was buried.

During the 1980s by dead of night a bunch of grave robbers dug up Honest Tom's remains and went down four foot without finding either horse or gold. At this point the headstone collapsed on top of the miscreants who ran off petrified.

There are no reported sightings of Issette's ghost yet!

7 Catching up with the Old Country

In her latter years, Issette occasionally wrote to the LGU to lambast 'those members whose only talent is for spending other people's money'. A reference to proposals that teams be sent abroad to gain experience, and to establish golfing links with other countries.

She also had reservations about the new biennial USA v Great Britain and Ireland competition for the Curtis Cup, even though it was hugely underwritten by the American Curtis Sisters to the tune of $5000 a match for the first ten years.

A match with America held few terrors for the sport's founders, because even going back to the days when the Curtis sisters were the American challenge, their girls had always been second best. The US game was still considered to be in its infancy, as it had only been founded in the 1880s when the 'wild west' dominated accounts of American life.

Everyone in Britain had heard of notorious outlaws, such as the Jesse James Gang, but few people had heard of the Apple Tree Gang of New York, and they too were making history and having trouble with the law.

THE APPLE TREE GANG

In the tame east of America, a thousand miles from the 'wild west', the gas-lit front room of Mr and Mrs John Reid's house in New York was the first meeting room of the nation's earliest documented golf club. It was called St Andrew's, and the hostess Mrs Reid had the honour of becoming America's first recorded lady golfer.

In February 1888 her husband had met a Scots linen merchant, Robert Lockhart of Dunfermline, who twelve months before had bought some golf clubs and balls from Old Tom Morris' shop in the old grey town of St Andrews. Using this single set of equipment, the Reids, Lockhart and several friends established a three-hole course in a farmer's field off Broadway. A tree in the corner of the meadow was used to hang up their overcoats – an action that earned them the nickname of the 'Apple Tree Gang'. The New York Police had some rather harsher names for them, for Lockhart was soon arrested for endangering the lives of the sheep that shared the 'links'.

Another US golfing pioneer, Alexander Baillie from Brechin in Scotland, also ran into trouble with the authorities when San Francisco Customs impounded his clubs and balls as 'dangerous looking weapons'.

TIN POT OCCUPATIONS

Such incidents were unusual, as golf rapidly gained popularity amongst the wealthy socialites of New York, Boston and Philadelphia. These people tended slavishly to copy the habits of the British upper class (even though their grandfathers had ejected the British during the War of Independence).

As golf was now the new major sport of the British upper classes, it was bound to spread to America. And in contrast with the other side of the Atlantic, women played a prominent part in founding the sport. They even established their own courses at Shinnecock Hills and Morristown.

By employing the best Scottish professionals to design and build new courses, the game rapidly took root in the New World. By 1894 there were 90 courses in the USA and a meeting was held in New York at which delegates from the principal clubs formed the United States Golf Association. Amongst the delegates was one Laurence Curtis of Brookline GC who indirectly had a great infuence on ladies' golf. The new clubs charged relatively high subscriptions to their members, but sufficient cash was rarely passed on to the professionals. They had to resort to pennypinching to complete their work, often using empty tin cans turned upside down as holes.

BEATRIX AND THE DIRTY TRICKS

1895 saw the men's United States Golf Association organising the first US Women's National Championship over two rounds of nine holes at Meadow Brook Golf Club, NY. The winner, Mrs C S Brown from Shinnecock Hills Golf Club, had the best score of 132 for 18 holes.

Mrs Brown proved to be a 'one win wonder'. She was replaced by a more enduring champion, Beatrix Hoyt (1880–1963), who became America's first notable lady golfer by winning the next three US titles. Miss Hoyt was, like all the entrants in the early days, a prim and proper young lady from a wealthy East Coast family.

Beatrix's first US Women's victory was at Morris County, New Jersey. This course had been awarded the Women's National Championship because it had been created, and was run, by women. But by the day of the event, the course's female founders had been deposed from the club committee after some unseemly manoeuvring by their husbands. Despite the mutterings of discontent at the coup d'état, Miss Hoyt stepped up to receive a large, ornate trophy donated by Scots Member of Parliament, Robert Cox, who had laid out the original nine-hole course for the now-departed ladies.

In 1899 Beatrix Hoyt helped found the Women's Metropolitan Golf Association which sought to emulate the LGU's control of ladies' golf in the North Eastern states. Although the WMGA held their own championships, control of the ladies' game remained with the male dominated USGA and

Ireland's May Hezlet considered this situation to be preposterous and commented, 'What can 160 men do for women's golf?'

Beatrix Hoyt worked hard for ladies' golf, on and off the course, until 1900. Then she suffered a shock defeat from a Boston girl, Margaret Curtis, in the Women's National at Shinnecock Hills, NY. In a fit of pique Beatrix retired to concentrate on becoming a painter and sculptress.

GOLFING COUSINS

Margaret was the youngest of the ten Curtis children of Beacon Hill, Boston, and second cousin of Laurence Curtis, who had helped form the USGA. Laurence had sent his cousins a copy of the Badminton Library's 'Golf' which had inspired the children to form a club at nearby Manchester-on-Sea which became known as the Essex Country Club. It became one of America's finest courses and Manchester's principal asset and employer.

Margaret was already a veteran of four Women's Nationals and had been 4th in 1897 when as a rather unfurnished youth of thirteen, she had looked distinctly uncomfortable with four clubs to carry around the course. She did not win the major title until 1906 but her name was forever associated with women's golf.

WOMEN DRIVERS

Miss Curtis lost that year's final to another girl who also contributed to golfing history. This was Frances Griscom a small but solidly built girl from Merion Cricket Club, Philadelphia.

Miss Griscom was golf's earliest 'tomboy' and was the first girl in golf history to drive herself to competitions in one of the 'new fangled automobiles'. Her driving from the tee on the golf course was popular and her home club marked her win by giving her a silver cup. 65 years later, as a grey-haired old lady, she returned it to them at their centenary celebrations.

Back in 1903 the young Francis broke new ground by persuading her friend Genevieve Hacker to join her in a trip to Britain to challenge for the British title. Neither girl made a great impact in Britain, but a meeting with the British Champion Lottie Dod led to the Hoylake girl visiting Philadelphia and playing in the US Championships. This set the trend that was to ultimately change the entire face of the sport.

THE CURTIS COUPLE

Lottie Dod did not play well in the US Championship, but matters were a lot more successful off the course. She persuaded Margaret Curtis and her sister Harriot to bring an American team to Britain for the 1905 LGU Championship at Royal Cromer and to play a match against a British team.

Margaret Curtis was just resuming golf after two years out with illness which had disrupted her school work. The school authorities were unhappy

ABOVE *British Championships, Royal Cromer, 1905. America's Harriot Curtis drives from the first tee with Tommy Miller Jnr in the background*

OPPOSITE TOP *1905, Cromer. Issette Pearson seated amid the British Championship competitors including the first ever US team of visitors*

RIGHT *Margaret Curtis drives from the 12th tee during the British Championships at Royal Cromer, 1905*

The second competition between USA and GB and Ireland, Royal County Down, Newcastle, in 1907

to hear that this strong-minded young lady planned to miss her final college examinations to visit Britain. When Margaret's final graduation papers arrived post-marked 'England', the college authorities refused to accept them and insisted Miss Curtis resume another year at college.

None of the US team could make much impact at Cromer, but the Curtis girls in particular were champion golfers in America. The elder girl Harriot Curtis (1881 – 1974), won the US Women's title in 1906 and was runner-up a year later to Margaret (1883 – 1965), who also won the US Title in 1908, 1911 and 1912. Margaret was always the more sturdily built of the two and was the better all-round athlete, having been 1908 US Tennis Doubles champion.

From a wealthy altruistic family, the Curtis sisters always had time for charitable work, but it is for their life-long support of Anglo-American golf that they are best remembered. In view of their subsequent services to British golf, it was rather cruel that the sisters' grip on the US Women's title was loosened by two visitors who clearly demonstrated the wide gulf between British and American ladies' golf at the start of the century.

ARE YOU A PLAYER MA'AM?

Apart from Lottie Dod's visit in 1903, Dorothy Campbell-Hurd (1883 – 1945) was the first British girl to seriously challenge for the North American Championships.

A lively, well-humoured girl, Dorothy had won the 1909 British Championship at Birkdale in a final that had ended rather prematurely, nearly a mile from the clubhouse. On the walk back, she became detached from the officials. When she finally arrived at the clubhouse door, the commissionaire barred her way and asked 'Are you a golfer, ma'am?' The champion replied, 'Not really but I will have to collect the winner's trophy anyway.'

Dorothy was never under the illusion that she was the most stylish or graceful golfer around, but, after receiving the customary invitation to play in America, she demonstrated the difference between the nations by winning that year's US and Canadian titles.

During her visit, she won many trophies but lost her heart to the new land and after a few initial reservations about the winter snow and broiling summers of Canada, Dorothy turned her back on Britain forever, married a local and settled in Hamilton, Ontario.

After the First World War, her best form deserted her but she worked at remodelling her swing and was rewarded with a second US Women's title at 41 years of age. Like the mellow whisky of her homeland, she improved with age. She broke 70 for the first time playing over men's tees in her 50s and is estimated to have won 750 competitions. She was tragically killed by a railway engine at Philadelphia station in 1945.

The great Dorothy Campbell (Hurd), winner of the US, Canadian and British Championships in a fifty-year career

In her prime, Dorothy had outclassed the best American girls and brought home to America that their girls trailed the best of the British. A salutory lesson that was repeated by a tall, bosomy girl from the Wirral.

BRITISH LIONS

Gladys Ravenscroft (1888 – 1960) was the daughter of a Liverpool wine merchant. As a teenager she was a top-class hockey player, and then she was persuaded to concentrate on golf.

In 1912 she won the British title at Turnberry. She defeated Cecil Leitch in a semi-final that went to four extra holes before Gladys sank a huge putt to clinch victory in one of best matches ever played in the history of the championship. The final against England international Stella Temple proved easy meat for Gladys. Inspired by Dorothy Campbell's success, Gladys decided to visit the 'new world' of golf.

The schedule arranged by her hosts was an arduous six-month tour of America's entire East Coast. Accompanying her were two other British girls, Muriel Dodd and Violet Harrison. Again the visitors demonstrated the quality of British ladies' golf.

Muriel Dodd beat Gladys in the final of the Canadian Ladies' Championship, but Gladys won the US Women's National at Wilmington, Delaware, beating the American No 1 Marion Hollins of Chicago in the final.

Only poor Miss Harrison failed to land a major prize. This caused one American newspaper to remark: 'She was the only lion who did not take a Christian.' This echoed the sentiment that America's top prizes would be easy pickings for the visitors until a truly great homegrown newcomer came along.

A GOOD OL' GIRL ENDS THE
GOOD OL' DAYS

The first generation of American lady golfers were rather genteel specimens who may have led the world in charm, but they trailed the visitors in chipping and putting. Almost all came from a claustrophobically similar background in the North Eastern states where all the major championships were organised.

However, it was from way down south in Georgia, where the magnolias blossom and the Spanish moss clings to the verandas of whitewalled clubhouses, that the first top-class US girl emerged. Alexa Sterling had a good golfing pedigree being the daughter of an ex-patriot Scots Doctor, and a childhood friend of the great men's champion, Bobby Jones. A world away from the golfing image of the first champions, Alexa was a likeable friendly soul with masses of southern charm until she walked on to the first tee. Then she became totally serious, with a great will to win. Not for her a gentle ladylike swing; she had grown up playing against men.

At an early age she had realised that you had to imitate the men's deliberate and mechanical club action if you were to get results.

As a teenager, her steely determination won a hat-trick of US Women's Championships and many good judges thought her the best in the world. In 1921 she was persuaded to make the long trip to Turnberry in Scotland for the British Championship to try to stem the tide of British invaders. Good fortune (and good weather) did not smile on this brave venture as she drew

Gladys Ravenscroft (LEFT) faces Cecil Leitch at Royal Portrush, 1911

US Women's National Championship – Glenna Collett and Thion de la Chaume

Cecil Leitch in the First Round. The morning sky was as black as night and rain was driving horizontally off the sea. The players, officials and 2,000 fiercely partisan home supporters suffered a terrible drenching. By halfway, Miss Sterling's heart began to ache for her native southern sunshine and her head became bowed. Thoroughly disheartened with life in the land of her ancestors, Alexa's swing disintegrated and defeat became inevitable.

Alexa vowed never to make the long journey to Europe again, and shortly afterwards married and moved to Ontario. In 1934, as Mrs Fraser, she became Canadian Champion.

Glenna Collett practises before the USA v GB match at Sunningdale, 1930

LITTLE LEAGUE TO WORLD SERIOUS

If Alexa had failed to win the British title, her achievements at home were firing the imaginations of a generation of teenage girls, who imitated her 'new swing' on the family lawns of North America. One girl in particular emerged to eclipse Alexa's record. This was Glenna Collett (1903–1988).

The small but powerful Miss Collett was press-ganged by her worried parents into taking up golf. Until she was thirteen she had devoted every spare moment to baseball. The switch from mound to golf tee brought spectacular results, for at eighteen she was US Ladies' Champion.

The experience of staring her baseballing boyfriends in the eye between pitches seemed to transfer easily to golf, for she became the greatest match-player of her era. In 1924 she lost only one match of sixty she played – and that was a fluke.

In the US Ladies' semi-finals she faced Mary Browne, who was a tennis champion and knew all about tight angles. The two girls were all square at the eighteenth with Glenna safely on the green, when Mary lost complete control of her drive sending the ball into the trees and seemingly bound for the next county. Suddenly the ball cannoned off a tree and bounced on to the green and straight into the hole! Not surprisingly, Mary's luck was now heavily overdrawn, and the venerable Dorothy Campbell beat her in the final.

OLD WORLD QUEST

Glenna Collett always laughed when she recounted the story but she had the consolation of winning a total of six US titles. Her greatest quest however seemed to elude her, for she competed regularly in the British Championship, but usually found Joyce Wethered too much for her, or anyone else.

Glenna and Joyce produced some of the greatest matches in the history of the championship, notably the 1929 final at St Andrews when the American girl started in a record 34 for the first nine and had a five stroke lead. Miss Wethered then produced a miracle finish to win at the 35th. 'That win gave me the greatest satisfaction of my whole career because my opponent played so well,' said the victor sixty years later.

A long-standing friendship developed between the tall, shy English girl and the tiny New Englander and Miss Wethered was one of the first house-guests of Glenna and her new husband Edwin Vare at their home in Vermont. The marriage was entirely appropriate, for Edwin was the longest driver in US men's golf and Glenna held that honour amongst the ladies.

Another moment of glory seemed to be in Glenna's grasp in 1930, at Formby, when she reached the final of the British Championship with no Joyce to bar the way. Instead her opponent was a tall talented teenager who seemed hopelessly out of her depth. This was Diana Fishwick, who was no pushover despite her youth. Back at her homeclub of North Foreland, the members would say 'You can be sure of only two things: income tax and Diana's name on the club prizelist.'

The impossible happened, and the teenage prodigy denied Glenna her final chance of the title. Fate had been cruel, but apart from the British title, Glenna had won every honour that the ladies' game had to offer. She was also to play a crucial role in one of her nation's finest victories which also turned out to be one of the game's major turning points.

8 Turning Points

An interested spectator at those memorable British finals of the 1920s was the former American champion Margaret Curtis, who had dropped out of golf at the start of the First World War and for a decade had done charitable work in Europe: first as head of the Red Cross Refugee Bureau and later handling a programme of child health which won her the Legion D'Honneur.

On her return to America in 1924 she resurrected the idea of regular Britain v USA matches and the following year raised the matter with the unenthusiastic British authorities.

Friendly matches were played between the two nations but only in 1927 was the go-ahead received from Britain for the contest to become official. It was another five years before the first match took place. With the benefit of hindsight, the reluctant maiden should have postponed the match forever.

NO CAUSE FOR CONCERN

But at the time, there seemed to be no reason for concern. Britannia had been top of the golfing pile since the 1890s, and everyone at home assumed that this state of affairs would continue. The only serious challenge had been a flourish of French success in the late 1920s, but that had been ended by Britain's triumph in the Vagliano Cup between Britain and France.

There did not appear to be a threat from across the Atlantic because America's best girls, such as Alexa Sterling and Glenna Collett, had generally disappointed on British soil. All previous, unofficial, matches between Britain and America had confirmed 'old world' supremacy, indeed such matches were regarded as mere 'time fillers' in championship week.

The last of the friendly matches was held in 1930, when Molly Gourlay's team defeated Glenna Colett's team from America 8-6. Enid Wilson recalls, 'What had begun as an informal occasion was written up so much by the Press and attracted such crowds that the general impression became that it was a full-scale international competition. From the interest aroused then, it was plain that the time was ripe for a formal contest.' It was then that Harriot and Margaret Curtis presented a cup inscribed 'TO STIMULATE FRIENDLY RIVALRY AMONG THE WOMEN GOLFERS OF ALL LANDS'.

A TEAM OF ALL THE TALENTS

British confidence was heightened when the team for the first Curtis Cup match in 1932 was announced. This was a team to beat all teams, and the selectors could not be faulted for picking the peerless Joyce Wethered, and surrounding her with players of the quality of Wanda Morgan, Diane Fishwick and Enid Wilson. This was perhaps the strongest side ever fielded in British ladies' golf history.

Wanda Morgan had started life determined to be a cricketer, until her parents had pointed out that Kent had never selected a girl and were probably never likely to. She opted for golf instead and became British Champion.

As good as Wanda was, the team's new star was the tall, sturdy girl from Derbyshire – Enid Wilson. Her search for personal excellence in everything she did, became a hallmark, of her life, be it as a writer, gourmet or golfer. Enid likes everything in its proper place, but she began life as a proper madam. She was expelled from school for swearing at a teacher who would not allow her to play golf. She shocked even more adults by winning the

'The team of all the talents' – the 1932 Great Britain team at Wentworth for the first Curtis Cup match

Derbyshire title at 15, and eventually a hat-trick of British titles.

As the British team arrived at Wentworth's turreted clubhouse, it seemed inconceivable that an American team of virtual unknowns could cause an upset.

PRIVATE PRACTICE

The American team was certainly full of unfamiliar names and few home supporters had heard of any of their players, except Glenna Collett.

The girls were 'unknowns' because they had been prevented from visiting Europe by the Great Depression, but some of these busy young ladies on the putting green were outstanding competitors – notably Virginia Van Wie (who was a triple US Women's Champion) and Maureen Orcutt (10 times winner of the highly competitive New York Metropolitan Championship).

It was also believed that the format of the new competition, which had a round of foursomes (followed by six singles), would work against the Americans as they very rarely played foursomes back at home; the British girls, on the other hand, had plenty of foursomes experience and had been

The 1932 American team for the first Curtis Cup, who created one of the game's great turning points

Virginia Van Wie (USA) in action in the 1932 Curtis Cup. She was to win three US National titles

especially strong in the foursomes round of the new Vagliano Cup match against France.

British confidence was so high that no attempt was made to keep the successful Vagliano Cup line-up. Indeed, the British team's whole preparation was casual. In Enid Wilson's opinion, it was 'Downright shameful. We were left alone to do what we wanted. If you did not want to practise, you did not have to.' To Enid, who thrived on practice, the whole operation was badly handled.

In contrast, American captain Marion Hollins worked her team hard for a full week, concentrating on foursomes and getting players accustomed to the pairings she planned to use in the match.

The competition began, and the home crowd was silenced. The unthinkable was happening. America won all three foursomes. There was something to cheer about in the singles, for Joyce Wethered, Enid Wilson and Diana Fishwick all won for Britain, but the foursomes deficit was irreversible. America had won 5½ – 3½.

As the porters packed the American bags, the Curtis sisters took special care of their Cup which had taken a generation to give away. The trouble was that no one had the sense to recognise the fact that the Americans may have taken the cup, but they had left behind a free lesson, in preparation, that it took Britain a generation to realise.

A DOWSING FROM CHEVY CHASE

Britain's first attempt to win the Curtis Cup on American soil came in 1934.

Despite the US money guarantee, the LGU approached the match with its customary stinginess and sent just enough players to field the team, and Doris Chambers as captain and reserve.

By contrast, the Americans spared no expense to ensure the success of the event. The course at Chevy Chase looked immaculate, and American officials scurried about seeing to every minor detail. They even persuaded the local militia, dressed in their best white uniforms, to act as crowd controllers. From the tee, the white uniforms stretched as far as the eye could see and looked remarkably like a picket fence. Sadly, a downpour left the militia absolutely sodden and their uniforms soon resembled "dress grey".

For the British girls, it was a wet, depressing experience for after sharing the foursomes, the singles went to America 5-1. Wanda Morgan, who played for Britain that day, still recalls the terrible weather and sitting on her bed, hours later, shivering with the cold and damp.

Enid Wilson, the new British champion in 1931 – great golfer, writer and gourmet

CLASS OF '36

With two matches played and two lost, the 1936 match gave the British selectors the chance to experiment with some of the exciting newcomers; Helen Holm, Pam Barton and Jessie Valentine.

The British team that arrived at Gleneagles had the look of a party of sixth formers on a school outing with their tweedy 'schoolma'am', Doris Chambers. Helen Holm, a beanpole of a girl, was already in her twenties. Pam Barton had not long left school before winning the 1936 British and US titles, and 'Wee Jessie' Valentine from nearby Perth had begun her golf with

RIGHT *Pam Barton winning the 1936 US National. Despite dismal results in the Curtis Cup, her victory brings home to the Americans that there is plenty of talent in Britain*

BELOW *The class of '36. Great Britain brings in some new youngsters and achieves an honourable draw in the 1936 Curtis Cup at Gleneagles*

Helen as her role model, but, she had soon replaced her heroine as the British Champion.

As Jessie was the local girl, the Gleneagles crowd made no secret of their feelings and cheered her every move. The cheering became mixed with a certain nervous tension when word filtered through that everything now rested on Jessie's young shoulders. She had to win to earn a draw for Britain.

At the final green, Jessie holed a 20ft foot putt to defeat her vastly more experienced opponent, Leona Cheney, and she became a national heroine.

STORM CLOUDS GATHER

Celebrations seemed a thing of the past by 1938 as Europe was sliding further into turmoil. Some voices argued that the Curtis Cup match at Essex Golf Club, Massachusetts, was inappropriate, but there had been written commitments and a British team was therefore despatched.

It was impossible for the players to forget the worsening situation. England's Elsie Corlett recalled that on the boat to America every possible space was occupied by refugees from Hitler's Europe. Being served at mealtimes was hard work, as the crew struggled to cater for the 3,000 passengers.

The British girls were certainly hungry for victory in the match. They won the foursomes 2½ – ½ and looked like tieing the match, until America's Charlotte Gutting took the last three holes in the final singles to take the Cup for the 'Stars and Stripes'.

On the boat home, the team were among only 50 passengers, this time being waited on by over 600 crew. Everybody was trying to leave Europe; nobody wanted to go there.

Back home, Elsie took the English title on the afternoon that Prime Minister Chamberlain returned from Munich with his famous appeasement document. Elsie remembered that only the players and officials ventured outdoors; everyone else stayed close to the wireless, anxious for news. 'After the war, everybody despised appeasement, but on that afternoon in 1938 everyone was delighted that war had been avoided.'

War was declared within twelve months, and the luxuries of life had to be put away. Golf clubs and great trophies went into cupboards where they would not be disturbed for years.

PARCELS FROM THE CURTIS SISTERS

One of the earliest victims of the war was Jessie Anderson's fiancé, George Valentine, who was taken prisoner during the fall of France. He was confined in a prisoner of war camp where conditions were atrocious and the Germans even refused to distribute Red Cross parcels.

Jessie wrote to Margaret and Harriot Curtis who had worked for the Red Cross in the 1920s and, thanks to the ladies' intervention, a regular supply of parcels began to reach George and the other prisoners.

9 Pam and Bunty

Until the fall of France in May, 1940, Britain treated the war as a minor irritant that would probably soon disappear. The catastrophic defeat of the Allies brought a sudden end to such an illusion.

At home, famous golfers of both sexes disappeared into the anonymity of khaki. Some great players distinguished themselves in uniform, none more so than Walker Cup player, Laddie Lucas, who led a squadron of Spitfires through the Battle of Britain.

OLD FRIENDS

One Autumn day in 1943, Laddie landed at RAF Manston in Kent where he was delighted to find an old golfing friend working at the aerodrome as a WAAF Officer. Pam Barton was equally pleased to see Laddy and the two arranged to have dinner that evening.

Over dinner, Laddie noticed the change in Pam, who had begun the war as a happy-go-lucky girl and was now a veteran of the blitz. She brightened up considerably when the talk turned to the good old days, when in the space of a couple of seasons she had gone from being an unknown to World Champion under the coaching of the great men's champion Archie Compston.

Archie was a tough task master, but he recognised a remarkable talent in this tiny freckle-faced youngster who could hit a golf ball a proverbial mile. Possessed of a great talent, Pam toured the world during the 1930s, winning the US Open and two British titles without losing a trace of her natural charm.

At home, one of Pam's less glamorous winter tasks was to visit courses to assess their standard scratch score which meant visiting places far removed from Royal Melbourne and Cape Town.

Everyone who met her, remembers her effervescent cheerfulness, exemplified by a memory from Tom Burton, who was the professional in the 1930s at Darwen out on the wild Pennine moors.

He recalls two ladies arriving one morning to assess the course and he was surprised to hear the smaller one give her name as 'Miss P Barton'. Everyone knew that she was the best woman player in the world. He said nothing

when she went out and played 18 holes before lunch, but afterwards, Pam Barton came back into the shop and said they would like to play another round and would he like to join them. The trio played off the men's tees and Tom recalls that the champion was a lovely, friendly girl who never stopped giggling and asking questions the whole way round.

Tom recalls he had to tell her off at one point. 'At every tee, she would ask me what was the best way to play the hole. In the end, I had to remind her that we had half-a-crown resting on the result and I didn't want to lose, even to a champion!'

A rare portrait of Pam Barton without a golf club in her hand, 1934

FAREWELL

Soon afterwards Pam joined the WAAF and three years saw her change from a young carefree girl into the experienced woman who sat opposite Laddie that evening. Laddie recalls that Pam had always refused to talk about golf

Cecil Leitch (beret) and Pam Barton at Ashridge GC, Hertfordshire. For some strange reason Cecil detested the young champion

over dinner before, but this time she was happy to reminisce.

Afterwards, Laddie and Pam said their farewells and departed. Laddie always maintains that Pam had a premonition that death was at hand and took this last chance to relive the golden days.

A week later Laddie learnt that Pam had been killed in an aircraft crash at Manston.

BUNTY'S STORY

The Second World War took the lives of many fine and brave young people and in the golfing world, no soul was more mourned than the brilliant Pam Barton. Her memory was especially cherished in America, and when in 1948 the future of the Curtis Cup was thrown into doubt by the LGU's financial problems, the Americans held 'Pam Barton Days' to raise the money needed to ensure that two teams could gather at Royal Birkdale.

With a decade since the last match, it was inevitable that both countries would be forced to field new names in their team, and many of the players would be unknown quantities. But at least the choice of Birkdale seemed to favour the British girls. The seaside links with its knee deep rough and hair-raising winds is a million miles from the manicured fairways and greens of American golf. Sadly the British girls seemed out of their depth, and the Americans won 6½ – 2½.

A TRADESMAN'S DAUGHTER

In the British camp there was much discontent about the selectors' decision to leave out Frances 'Bunty' Stephens. She was after all a top-class player and a member of Royal Birkdale. But, she was also the daughter of Fred Stephens, the Bootle professional, so her outstanding talent was ignored to preserve the snobbish requirements that the game's tradesmen (and their relatives) should be kept at arm's length.

Bunty retaliated by winning the next British Championship and two years later her claims were pressed at the highest level by the 70-year-old, former champion, Gladys Ravenscroft (Dobell). She organised a petition protesting about the girl's exclusion. Not surprisingly, the selectors backed down and picked young Bunty for the next Curtis Cup match away in Buffalo, New York.

Many stories have grown up about the relationship between Bunty and her father, suggesting that Fred cajoled Bunty into being the champion he had never been. One tale has it that Fred saw a newspaper report of Great Britain's 7½ – 1½ drubbing in Buffalo, which said Bunty's putting had let her down. As soon as Bunty arrived back at Bootle, Fred led her to the putting green and insisted that she practise for an hour before she could even unpack her bags.

This particular story seems unlikely, because Bunty won all Britain's

The 1948 Curtis Cup, Royal Birkdale. Britain's dismal performance forced the selectors to choose Bunty Stephens, who had to be content with being a spectator on her own links

points in Buffalo, and she herself was always determined to be a great player. On the occasion of her 21st birthday, Fred asked her how she wanted to celebrate. 'I'll settle for 18 holes with you' replied the youngster.

MUIRFIELD INCONVENIENCE

As Bunty had contributed all Britain's points in Buffalo, not surprisingly she kept her place for the 1952 match over the ancient links of Muirfield. This was a curious venue, because the Scots club has never allowed women to join and indeed no woman golfer had ever entered its portals.

Bunty's teammate, Jeanne Bisgood, remembers that the Curtis Cup teams changed across the road from the clubhouse, but on the Wednesday afternoon they were invited to tea by the 'Honourable Company of Edinburgh Golfers'. She thought this was a great honour, to be the first women ever to enter Muirfield, but then she read a large notice in the foyer. It said, 'The club committee regrets the inconvenience to members caused by admitting women to the building'.

Another British player remembers the terrible driving rain, and huddling in front of the clubhouse for shelter. She was watching Bunty Stephens as she attempted an important putt. Suddenly a member inside the clubhouse beckoned through a window. She assumed this was an invitation to shelter inside the clubhouse, and she happily went to the main door where the gentleman appeared and said, 'Do you mind not standing in front of the window, we can't see the match.'

As it turned out, Muirfield was the perfect venue for Great Britain as they won the foursomes 2 to 1, and then Bunty, Jeanne Bisgood and Elizabeth Price won their singles. Elizabeth Price was subject to the most strain in the final match. A diabetic, Miss Price was informed at the halfway point that victory rested on her shoulders. The match was all square at that point, but her opponent made errors at three consecutive holes to give the match to Great Britain and Ireland.

Afterwards the American Captain said ruefully, that the result would 'cause a stir back home'. The stir did not last long for America comfortably defeated Great Britain 6 – 3 in the next meeting.

CLOSE ENCOUNTERS

For the 1956 renewal at Sandwich, the US selectors were forced to pick an inexperienced team; by contrast Great Britain and Ireland had a settled side, an experienced captain in Zara Bolton, and were able to bring in a couple of talented youngsters including Angela Ward (Bonallack).

Despite Britian losing the foursomes, the singles were a triumph with Angela Ward, Elizabeth Price and Jessie Valentine all winning to tie the match. Bunty was still on the course, locked in combat with America's Polly Riley who had previously never been beaten in four Curtis Cup appearances.

Bunty Stephens was to put two large holes in Polly's record but only by the

narrowest of margins. This year, Polly was forced to concede on the 18th green, thereby giving Great Britain its second victory.

By a curious coincidence, Polly and Bunty found themselves in exactly the same position two years later at Brae Burn. The last pair on the course, the word was quietly passed on that a half for Polly would give victory to America. Everything hinged on one 20ft putt on the last green. Bunty Stephens had to sink it to defeat Polly. The only person present, without their heart in their mouth, was Bunty and she coolly lined up the putt and put it away.

LEFT Frances (Bunty) Stephens getting out of trouble

ABOVE The 1956 Curtis Cup at Prince's course, Sandwich. Polly Riley (left) concedes defeat on the 18th hole to Frances Stephens (Smith), giving Great Britain its second win. By coincidence the result was repeated in 1958 to give Britain a draw

THERE ARE NO HAPPY ENDINGS

Polly Riley and Bunty Stephens shook hands on Brae Burn's 18th hole knowing that this, for them, was their final Curtis Cup appearance. Shortly afterwards Bunty married airline pilot Roy Smith, and had a daughter, but weeks after the birth, news reached England that Roy had been killed in a plane crash in Africa.

Bunty carried on normally for several years, and even acted as an international selector, although her thin and consumptive nature was getting the upper hand. Gradually her health deteriorated and after 10 years of fighting illness she died of cancer in 1978.

The golf world mourned a fine champion and raised £20,000 to aid cancer sufferers at the hospital where she died.

10 Putting on a Brave Face

Despite the retirement of Bunty Stephens, the 1960s opened on a note of optimism for Britain when it produced perhaps the most unusual golfing talent of all time. She brightened up life for everyone she encountered. Her name was Marley Spearman and she seemed to contradict every known theory on golf evolution. But, sadly, for British golf, she was the light at the start of a long dark tunnel.

GENIUS IS BORN, NOT CREATED

The most widely accepted theory in golf is that you have to be born with a putter in your pram to develop quickly enough to make a top golfer. Marley Spearman, a 22-year-old dancer in London's West End, had never played golf at any level until one wet day, when she went into Harrods to buy a pound of smoked salmon and emerged to find there were no taxi-cabs. Whilst sheltering in the entrance, she spotted a sign which read, 'Golf School'. She went inside for a free lesson. As her husband and his friends were keen golfers, Marley thought a golf lesson would make an interesting conversation piece at the evening's dinner party.

The dinner guests may not have treated Marley's interest in the sport too seriously, but the next day she went to Holdwright's Golf Range in Regent's Park. Mr Holdwright asked what they could do for the tall, willowy lady in pig-tails and red trousers. 'It's all right, I learnt to play yesterday in Harrods,' replied Marley.

Tactfully, Mr Holdwright acknowledged that the lady had a natural swing, but said he might be able to bring about some slight improvement. In two years, Marley was down to four handicap when she entered the prestigious Worplesdon Foursomes and reached the final. Thus began a decade of incredible success which was not always fun and games. Marley attributes her success to 'The pleasure of playing the game and to the dedication to practise that her career as a dancer had taught her.'

Marley won two British Opens but does not recall a great deal about either occasion, but admits it was great fun at the time. She was always a brilliant foursomes player and in 1965, Marley recorded one of the most remarkable results in golf history when she partnered Brigitte Varangot to win the 72-

hole Casa Pupo Foursomes. Their winning margin was 21 strokes.

But by the mid-sixties it was time to exit as dramatically as the great lady had made her entrance. 'I always intended to quit at the top,' she says.

Marley Spearman, a natural who learned to play in Harrods

HEROINES OF THE DARK HOURS

For all her self-effacing good humour, Marley Spearman had a fine Curtis Cup record at a time when Britain was slipping into a 13-match losing sequence that lasted from 1960 to 1986.

Marley was one of a string of British girls who proved world class in competition and who even had good individual Curtis Cup records but could never get within shouting distance of success in the biennial team matches. Into this category come Ann Irvin, Mickey Walker, Mary Everard, Belle Robertson and a number of other unlucky girls. If the talent was available, what went so wrong in 1960 and continued for two decades?

ALL OUR TRIALS

There are many reasons why things went wrong for Britain's Curtis Cup teams. Some factors were beyond their control – notably the quality of the opposition, but many of the reasons were due to the 'amateurish' (in its worst possible context) approach of the home unions.

Throughout this 'dark age', the records of the previous Cup committee were destroyed so that the incoming captain would not be encumbered by other people's experiences and opinions. (This is a logic that argues experience is worthless and ignorance is bliss?)

If the captains had their problems, they were nothing compared to the problems of the players, who were driven to distraction by excessive demands and petty restrictions. Until the 1970s, every player was assessed on trial matches consisting of 10 rounds of matchplay against other 'possibles'. This process took a week to complete and told the selectors far less than a ten-minute examination of the national championship results. For players with work or family commitments, this meant finding excuses for 7 days of trials, 7 days of team practise and 7 days away to play in the actual match.

If three weeks away from home was worth the thrill of wearing the Curtis Cup blazer, the ludicrously strict interpretation of being an 'amateur' certainly was not. All the players were expected to pay their caddy themselves, and it was totally unthinkable to accept free golf balls offered by the bucketload from the manufacturers. In the end, several of the top players rebelled and the LGU had to relent. They therefore let them off the fiver for the caddy and allowed the acceptance of free balls.

But perhaps the golf balls themselves were the real reason for Britain's golfing decline.

LADDIE'S LAW

If British women's golf went downhill in the 1960s, the same could be said of the men's game. The arrival of US golfers of the quality of Arnold Palmer, Jack Nicklaus and Tom Watson marked an all time low for the home-produced players. If a British golfer was still in contention for the Open Championship by lunchtime on the first day, it was a major surprise. But Britain had brought the sport to the world and something had obviously gone wrong.

An astute observer of British golf is Laddie Lucas, an outstanding Walker Cup player and friend of many of the greatest players of modern times. He visited America in 1937 and played with the new, slightly larger, 1.68 inch golf ball that had just crept into their game.

'In Britain we used the 1.62 inch ball which suited the naturally wristy way our game had always been played. Strong wrists, it was said between the wars, were a great asset for a golfer. But American courses are different to ours because they are composed largely of Bermuda grass which clings tenaciously to a golf ball. The smaller ball tended to get buried, which is why the bigger ball was adopted; it is just so much easier to hit out of Bermuda grass.

Because the big ball was easier to hit, it encouraged the American golfers of both sexes to become better strikers of the ball. However it takes a generation from when you abandon the small ball for players to develop that improvement; the Americans adopted the bigger ball in the 1930s and only began to emerge as world champions in the late 1950s and 1960s.

In Britain we only accepted the new ball in 1962 and it took 20 years before players like Sandy Lyle, Laura Davies and Nick Faldo emerged as world class – at the same time that the girls began to pose a threat again to the Americans in the Curtis Cup.'

THE VIEW FROM THE WINNER'S CIRCLE

Perhaps the final word on why America should run up 13 straight wins belongs to perhaps the greatest player to ever represent either side. Anne Sander played for the USA as a teenager and was recalled in 1990 as a 53-year-old. How did America struggle for parity in the 1950s and then suddenly leave Great Britain behind for a golfing generation?

'I made my debut in 1958 and my special memory is sitting on the grass surrounding the 18th hole and watching Bunty Stephens and Polly Riley fighting out their match. Even then, you knew that it would have historical significance because it obviously affected the result and there were two of the greatest players in the history of the sport, reaching the last green in their last Curtis Cup match.'

Lindrick, 1960. The US captain, Mrs H. Prunaret, with the Curtis Cup. Anne Sander is second from the left in the front row

But that afternoon spelt the beginning of total domination of the Cup by America. Why did Anne Sander think that had happened? 'It was a fluke. British golf did not go into decline. It was just that the number of players in America grew and grew from the mid-fifties onwards. And in the US team we were lucky to have a core of career amateurs such as Barbara McIntire, JoAnne Gunderson and Trish Preuss who were available for a considerable time and provided the backbone of those winning sides.

Nobody can predict when or where successful players will emerge. JoAnne Gunderson and I both came from the same part of Washington State and between us won six of seven US Amateur Titles. Washington State is not noted for producing golfers.'

But how did Anne get started?

'I'm not from a golfing family. My father owned a golf course but he had never played. He knew enough about his average customer to make sure there were no bunkers on the course.'

Any conversation with Anne naturally has to include the obvious question. 'Why did she not follow JoAnne Gunderson and turn professional?' 'I was teaching and really enjoyed my work, plus I was happy to play six or so competitions a year. You can't be a professional on six tournaments a year! And later on I had my three boys, so I was happy to stay an amateur.

Being an American amateur does not instantly make you a celebrity. In America, the Curtis Cup has a low profile and has only been televised twice – in 1974 and 1990. It's different in Britain where everyone knows about the Curtis Cup. I lived over there for five years during the 1970s and I know your best players have some unusual weather to cope with, not like the girls in California. In Scotland with the winds, I had to develop a sort of reverse pivot style of driving from the tee but the funny thing was that more Scots people recognised me as a Curtis Cup player than ever at home.

Some things could be difficult in Britain, though. I once spent an hour asking people in London where Beauchamp Place was, until I found out you call it Beecham Place for some reason!'

THE ONLY WAY IS UP

By the early 1980s the Americans had won a dozen successive Curtis Cup matches and voices were starting to suggest that the competition was too one-sided to continue.

Pressure for change in the format began to grow when the men professionals' Ryder Cup was rescued from oblivion by fielding a European team in preference to a purely British team. Surely the ailing Curtis Cup was worthy of similar treatment?

Maybe the threat of foreign intervention was the vital spark that marked the end of the dark age of British women's golf. The 1984 match proved a nail-biter, being settled by a solitary singles win in America's favour. Possibly a better reason for the improvement in British fortunes, was the appointment of a new captain in Diane Bailey.

But what had happened to suddenly stop the rot and why was a new captain so significant.

Diane says 'People misunderstand the role of the Curtis Cup captain. She does not pick the team – that's the responsibility of a committee selected by the home countries. The captain's role is somewhere between friend and controller to the players and someone who must engender team spirit from the whole group, obviously making sure discipline is right.

My only problem in the early days was getting the girls to realise that the Americans were not invincible just because they had won for nearly 30 years and also to get them to believe in themselves. If the girls could get round in par, that would be enough to beat the Americans.

Obviously the 1986 match was going to be difficult as it was away, in Kansas. The temperature there can reach 100 degrees and dehydration becomes a serious problem. I consulted several doctors who had advised our Olympic athletes and they warned that our girls could lose up to 5lb in body fluids during 18 holes. Dehydration would cause our girls to struggle over the last two or three holes which could be enough to lose us the point, so we introduced a system for the British team that they had to take drinks frequently during a round, rather like marathon runners.

Another area where I felt improvement was needed was the image of the team. They were carrying the hopes of the whole country and deserved a good send-off, smart uniform and good accommodation.'

Victorious Curtis Cup captain Diane Bailey tries to keep in touch during the 1988 match

VICTORY AT PRAIRIE DUNES

Inspired by their first-class treatment, the British girls of 1986 were the first British golf team, male or female, professional or amateur, ever to win in America.

Matters began superbly with a 3-0 victory for Great Britain and Ireland in the foursomes where a blend of experience and talented youth worked wonders. The combination of steady, experienced Jill Thornhill with the new Irish champion Lilian Behan romped to a huge 7 and 6 win, one of the largest wins in the competition's history.

In the afternoon singles, the Behan-Thornhill success story continued and another newcomer Trish Johnson won at the top of the scoresheet.

The second day continued the magic with Miss Johnson winning her singles, and also her foursomes in company with Wales's Karen Davies, who also went undefeated through the match. The resounding 13-5 win was not just about the new players, however. It was a triumph for girls like Belle Robertson, Vicki Thomas and Mary McKenna, who had performed admirably throughout the dark age of British ladies' golf and emerged to sample the joy of victory.

CHANNEL WEATHER

Two years later there was an interesting omen for the British team. Great

In the 1988 Curtis Cup at Royal St George's Britain's Linda Baymon got a half with a spectacular 35-yard putt to retain the trophy

Britain and Ireland's captain, Diane Bailey, had defeated her American equivalent Judy Bell in a Curtis Cup match way back in 1962.

The weather gods smiled on the British team when four days of practice at Royal St George's, Sandwich were played in perfect seaside sunshine. This turned into a howling Channel gale for the first day of the competition. The Americans never came to terms with the weather. When they donned their weatherproofs and went out on to the course, the sun came out; when they wore their summerwear, it poured with rain again. Accustomed to the vicissitudes of the British weather, the British girls knew just what to expect and coped better.

After an encouraging 2–1 start in the foursomes, Linda Bayman, Julie Wade and Susan Shapcott all won at the top of the order to guarantee Britain a first day lead.

Day two saw Britain survive the second foursomes without losing a point. All that was needed was a half in Linda Bayman's match against Teri Kerdyk to retain the trophy. She got the half with a spectacular 35 yard putt at the 18th.

If the British were becoming accustomed to winning the Curtis Cup trophy, the American decision to restore Anne Sander to their 1990 team should have been a warning that there could soon be a large gap in the trophy cabinet. Mrs Sander had never really forgiven Great Britain for ruining her debut back in 1958, and in the interim years had piled on the misery by being the cornerstone of wins over Great Britain and Ireland.

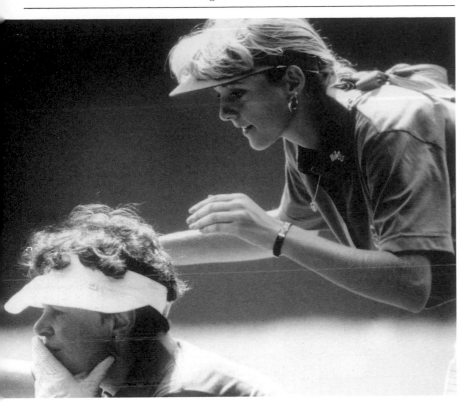

At 53, the oldest player in Curtis Cup history, Anne Sander was paired in the 1990 First Day Foursomes with the youngest ever player, 16-year-old wonder kid Vicki Goetze. Anne Sander says, 'Funnily, our partnership worked well, because Vicky and I were the shortest drivers on either side so we thought along the same lines.'

The magic worked, giving the USA a winning start in a match which was always going one way. Great Britain and Ireland were trailing 6–3 after day one and the American machine dropped only one point on day two for a crushing 14-4 victory.

The youngest player in Curtis Cup history, Vicki Goetze, and the oldest, Anne Sander. The 1990 Curtis Cup, Somerset Hills, New Jersey

A DIFFERENT WORLD

The Curtis Cup still represents a major challenge for Great Britain and Ireland, to wrestle the bowl from the 'new world'. But in America, women's amateur golf has a much lower profile since the emergence of women's professional golf.

For any top class American girl amateur, the logical next step is to turn professional and the success of American professional women's golf has begun a chain reaction throughout Europe and the Far East. Now girl golfers can earn millions of dollars a year, but it has not always been so.

As a handful of courageous women created the amateur game, the success of the professional game is due to a few brave young women who chose a different path from their peers.

Part Two

1 The American Dream

It is a misconception that lady professionals are a new breed of super-girls. In the 19th century, a small number of women earned a living from golf. These were the wives or daughters of Scots professionals, and they helped the breadwinner by club making, repairing equipment or giving lessons to lady amateurs.

In 1898, Issette Pearson devoted a chapter of her book *Our Lady of the Green* to advice for aspiring lady professionals. Issette was also friendly with May Dunn at Wimbledon before May's move to America.

It was, however, the 1930s before the foundation of the present professional ladies' game was established with the banishment from the amateur ranks by the USGA of several girls who had earned money playing other sports. Mary K Browne (who had defeated Glenna Collett Vare in 1924) was banned for having received money during her days as a tennis player. The major catalyst was a Texan girl who was to change the golfing world. Her name was Mildred Didrikson, better known as 'Babe Zaharias'.

THE BABE

At 19, Mildred's supernatural talents as an athlete catapulted her from the obscurity of an insurance office to the winner's podium of the Olympic Stadium in Los Angeles, where in 1932 she set three world records in the javelin and hurdles. She was also first in the high jump but was disqualified for using the Western roll (which was later accepted as legitimate).

Reluctant to return to an office, Babe decided sport might offer an alternative source of income, and despite her average height she proved above average at basketball, tennis, diving, roller skating and baseball, where five home-runs in one match earned her comparison with the great Babe Ruth and an enduring nickname.

Persuaded to take up golf, Babe won the second event she entered, the Texas Women's Invitational. But she was soon in trouble with the USGA, who classed her as professional for having earned money from basketball and baseball.

Ever ready to exploit a good headline, Babe used the resulting furore to stimulate interest in a series of matches against England's Joyce Wethered and the great Gene Sarazen, who had just won both the US and British Opens. Despite Babe's inexperience, she could outdrive Gene Sarazen at four of 18 holes, but as her defeats by Miss Wethered proved, Babe had an indifferent short game.

The legendary golf teacher Tommy Armour was hired to overcome the deficiency, but he found the Babe obsessed with power play. A story of their first lesson attributes Armour with the opening gambit:

'What are your tactics on the course, Mildred?'
'I just hit the ball at the pin, Mr Armour.'
'And what happens then?'
'Not much, chipping and putting are easy.'
'Well, if it's that easy, let's see you do it for a change.'

Tommy brought the required improvement but the outbreak of the Second World War diminished the prospects of earning a living from golf. Babe had become isolated outside the amateur ranks with two former US champions, Helen Hicks and Patty Berg (who specialised in giving women's golf clinics). With no income and no competition, Babe decided to reapply for amateur status which the USGA granted in 1943.

Babe Zaharias, winner of the 1947 British Championship at Gullane

COMING IN FROM THE COLD

Under her married name of Mrs Zaharias, Babe won the 1946 US Women's National and a year later she travelled to Scotland for the British Championship at Gullane. Babe's uninhibited approach to life and golf shocked the British public.

The great Enid Wilson, who was at the time working as a journalist, wrote, 'On a still day she went over the 15th green with her second shot, for which she took a number four iron. This hole is 540 yards, the first 400 being level ground and the last 140 uphill. This, on soft ground.'

Enid added, 'She adored the limelight and loved to wisecrack with the gallery. As a show woman she has no equals.'

Jean Donald, who lost to Babe in the semi-finals, saw a different side. She recalled that the wisecracking was part of Babe's act designed to attract headlines and attention; in private Babe was a most sporting and gracious opponent.

BACK IN THE OLD ROUTINE

After Gullane, Babe reverted to being a professional and hired ex-US PGA Tournament director Fred Corcoran as her manager. Fred worked closely with Wilson's, the sports equipment manufacturers, who had promoted golf clinics by Patty Berg and Helen Hicks before the war and were keen to set up a women's professional tour. A women's tour had been started in 1944 but had simply faded away due to lack of interest.

Fred arranged a meeting with Wilson's, Patty Berg and Babe Zaharias,

ABOVE *Babe Zaharias (left) and Jean Donald at the 1947 British Championship. Jean said that Babe was a most sporting and gracious opponent, but a great show-off*

RIGHT *Patty Berg in Britain with the US Ladies' Professional Tour, 1951*

which inaugurated the 'Ladies Professional Golf Association' with a tour schedule of three events in 1949. By 1951 the list had expanded to 21.

WITH A LITTLE HELP FROM OUR MEN FRIENDS

It was Corcoran's association with Alvin Handmacher, a women's sports clothes manufacturer, that really got the LPGA underway. A series of tournaments called the 'Weathervane Transcontinental' was moved across America with Handmacher guaranteeing $15,000 prize money per tournament and paying Babe $10,000 a year to wear his clothes.

Fred Corcoran said later, 'Without Alvin Handmacher and his Weathervane championships there would not be a women's pro tour. Alvin put the Ladies' PGA in business. But it was Babe Zaharias who made it go. She was the colour, the gate attraction and perhaps the greatest woman athlete the world has ever seen.'

By the time the final Weathervane tournament was played in 1953, Babe was seriously ill with cancer. America loved her before, but now her fight for life through a series of operations made her a national heroine. Even in adversity she remained irrepressible and she played harmonica on a gramaphone record and promoted the disc on the Ed Sullivan Show.

She died in September 1956 and remarked at the end, 'All my life, I've always had the urge to be better than everyone else.' She died aged 42 having lived up to her ambition.

BETSY'S BEGINNINGS

If Babe always seemed to be top of the pops in her lifetime, it was partly an illusion. Like all the early LPGA players, Babe had to struggle to overcome the opposition to the new tour. Betsy Rawls was another of the early LPGA stars and she recalls those days were hard work. 'You couldn't make money at it. We practically had to beg people to turn professional. If you played pro golf then, you must have really loved the game.'

Betsy loved the game, but she had plenty of reason, for within six months of turning professional, she won the 1951 US Women's Open. 'My problem was that I actually thought winning great titles was easy. In later years I became more realistic. By the highest standards I was never a great hitter, but I had the short game to make up.

I think we had a better attitude in those early days because we spent every moment we could on the course. The practice ground has its place but only by playing frequently can you develop the whole game. Modern players spend so much time on the practice ground, they tend to forget that golf is about getting from tee to green in the minimum number of strokes.'

Betsy thinks it is wrong to underestimate the quality of the players in those early days. 'Patty Berg and Louise Suggs were great players. It is a mistake to think they were big fish in a small pond.' Indeed Patty won 44 professional titles between 1948 and 1962, including the US Women's Open.

Betsy, Patty and Louise were the big stars until a blond, blue-eyed kid from California emerged to challenge everyone.

THE ALL-AMERICAN GIRL

Mary Kathryn (Mickey) Wright was an infant golfing prodigy who never allowed golf to interfere with her studies. But after gaining a degree in psychology, she turned professional and began 15 years of uninterrupted success, amassing 82 tour wins.

She was a huge hitter by even the most modern standards, and possessed a mechanical swing that never let her down. She won four US Women's Opens – a record she shares with Betsy Rawls – and four LPGA Championships, despite the phenomenal growth of the game in the post-war years. There was tough opposition from girls like Carol Mann and in particular Kathy Whitworth.

PRACTICE MAKES PERFECT

Kathy never had Mickey Wright's swing or Betsy Rawls' escapology, but she could always put together a good score regardless of conditions. The elegant Texan is reputed to have never played two consecutive bad rounds in 20 years of LPGA competition; this consistency of play brought a record 88 Tour wins. But Kathy Whitworth had no magic secret. She turned professional at 18 and had struggled for four years until constant practice reduced her average by six strokes and finally brought her eight tour wins in 1963.

Kathy Whitworth, perhaps the most consistent woman player in the sport's history

TIMES, THEY ARE A-CHANGING

Kathy Whitworth was the first of a new breed who had not served a lengthy amateur apprenticeship. To America's young girls, the LPGA champions were now the stars that Glenna Collett and Alexa Sterling had been to an earlier generation.

The change in opinion was due to the success of the men's game and television. The two major US television channels had fought for years over who would cover the men's PGA tournaments each weekend. The company who failed to cover the men's tournament retaliated by showing the last day of the US Women's Open in 1963. Gradually, showing the women's game became a weekly event. At first the viewers were slow to switch channels but after a while, the female game was attracting 40 per cent of the men's audience. The advertisers were quick to spot the potential.

CLEAN CUT

The Colgate-Palmolive company was keen to be associated with any area which could promote good hygiene with the massive female market. It promoted the film star Dinah Shore as the perfect American woman – clean, tidy and healthy. Dinah was in fact a keen golfer and Colgate tried a series of televised Dinah Shore Pro-Ams, pairing the glamour of ladies' golf with Hollywood stars such as Dinah, Bob Hope and Bing Crosby.

The viewing figures were excellent and Dinah Shore became part of the LPGA scene, eventually having her own major competition. Ladies' professional golf in America was becoming chic, highly visible and was establishing itself as a major force in the sport.

The big courses, that had originally refused the LPGA access, now recognised their folly. They were joined by the major golfing authorities, such as the USGA which took over the Women's Open. Appropriately, their first championship in 1963 at Rochester GC, NY, went to Betsy Rawls – the first woman to serve on their rules' committee.

MOVING OBJECTS

However, all was not perfect, for few girls were earning sufficient money to justify the lifestyle. Ordinary matters, such as home life and friends, were sacrificed to keep up with the constant demands of meeting tournament schedules. What money was on offer as prizes was soon absorbed by the travelling costs. This deterred many players from taking the big step into the professional world and right through the 1960s, players such as JoAnne Carner (Gunderson) stayed amateur.

BIG MOMMA

JoAnne from Kirkland, Washington, compiled one of the finest amateur records, claiming five US Amateur wins. Nicknamed 'Big Momma', JoAnne is of only average height, but being powerfully built she is a mighty hitter of a golf ball. Eventually in 1970 she took the professional plunge at the age of 30 and, accompanied by husband/manager Don Carner, drove the thousands of miles between events in a 'dormobile' which also acted as home. Despite the hardship, at 32 she became the oldest 'Rookie of the year' in LPGA history and finished 11th in the money winners' list. She went on to win two US Opens among 42 Tour victories.

Within four years, JoAnne had become the No 1 ranked player and finished top again in 1982 and 1983, even though she is a player who, by her own admission, specialises in 'birdie-bogey' scoring. She fights hard to control the urge to blast the ball, saying 'I just never know where the ball will end up.'

NANCY

The girl who proved the next spark to the LPGA was Nancy Lopez, a meteor of a talent who dominated US Ladies' golf in the late 1970s. After a brief but successful amateur career, Nancy turned professional in 1978.

With her self-taught style, the Californian girl seemed an unlikely world beater. 'I have a slow deliberate swing because I have seen many golfers with small swing errors that become catastrophic because they swing at breakneck speed.'

Breakneck describes her success as a professional. Nine tour wins in her rookie season (including five-in-a-row) preceded 1979 when she won the third of the tournaments she entered. But as quickly as she emerged, she seemed to fall away again. The perfect slow swing had developed a hook and

BELOW LEFT JoAnne Gunderson (Carner). Despite a long amateur career, JoAnne has become an outstanding professional in America

BELOW Nancy Lopez – back to her brilliant best

the good days seemed over. But a second marriage in 1982 to baseball star, Ray Knight, and motherhood, provided the answer to her swing problems that the golf experts could not find. The good times returned and in 1985, she set a new moneywinning record and was Player of the Year for the third time.

A fourth Player of the Year title came in 1988, and yet more trophies for the family home in Pecan, Georgia, as she brought her Tour victories to 44. When at home, Nancy lists her hobbies as running the kids to school, but Ray's retirement from baseball enabled Nancy to devote more time to competition, culminating in her first LPGA Championship win in 1990.

PARALLELS

Nancy Lopez's phenomenal success in the 1970s was mirrored by the massive success of Jack Nicklaus in the men's game, and by a curious coincidence as a period of parallel development slipped into both men's and women's golf. When Jack Nicklaus' years of total domination came to an end in the 1980s, no single giant stepped forward to grasp the golden putter. A dozen top-class players are now fighting for domination.

When Nancy Lopez's swing problems ended her early domination of game, again no single individual emerged to completely dominate women's golf, although a dozen major female names have filled the void.

NEW HEROINES

Amy Alcott started off in the game by destroying her father's lawn. She sank empty baked bean cans to imitate holes. He built her a sand bunker, but he must have felt like jumping into it when Amy's stray shots started smashing the windows. Dad provided a huge net to counteract this threat and, throughout the 1980s, Amy has been a threat to any lady golfer in the world. She started off as a top amateur but has refused all offers of new golf clubs, preferring to use the same old set. But this old set has brought her 29 tour wins, including the 1980 US Women's Open.

Other players' aspirations have been affected by illness: Sandra Haynie won 42 tournaments until arthritis ended her career, and Pat Bradley with 27 tour wins, including the US Open, developed thyroid trouble, which kept her off the Tour for a year.

Pat Sheehan had a choice between skiing and golf. Golf won, and despite being tiny by golf standards, she has won 5 events, two of them LPGA Championships – the second by 10 strokes.

The tall and willowy Beth Daniel is the tour's biggest hitter and perhaps the most outstanding modern woman player. She began as a PE graduate and won two US Amateur Championships before turning professional in 1979. She won her first event as a rookie and in 1980 she claimed seven tour wins. Perhaps Beth's principal rival is Betsy King, a born-again Christian, who won the US Women's Open in 1989 and in 1990 became only the fourth player to win the title in successive years. In 1989 she became Player of the Year for the second time and claimed her 24th tour victory in 1991.

These girls have won sporting headlines, but one LPGA player has won headlines for all the wrong reasons. Although the LPGA authorities are not enamoured by her antics, she has become a legend throughout women's golf.

MUFFIN THE MULE

Muffin Spencer-Devlin from Florida, has gained a notoriety far beyond her 3 tour wins in the 1980s. Her fame stems from an unusual lifestyle which has included applying to become an astronaut, and championing reincarnation.

Muffin was the victim of a difficult upbringing, becoming involved in drug abuse at college before beginning a brief career as a model and actress. She rapidly switched ambitions in the mid-1970s and, despite modest achievements on the course, decided to become a top golfer by applying to the LPGA Qualifying School as a 2 handicapper (the ink must have run out before the second digit). At the fourth attempt she made the grade and began another four years of struggling as a tour professional before winning the first of her tournaments.

Despite her bizarre behaviour, Muffin is a superlative golfer when things go right. At Knollwood, NY, in 1986, she broke the world record with 28 for 9 holes. Unfortunately she often makes headlines for the wrong reasons, such as listening to pop music on a 'walkman' whilst playing in a tournament. She wore cycling shorts for competitions and fired three caddies in four rounds. Her best-documented escapade was damaging the LPGA's clean-cut image by turning up half-cut at a dinner for the European Ford Classic. On being informed she could not be able to sit at the top table, she offered the WPG Executive, Joe Flanagan, some advice on his private life. 'I've not heard language like that since I left the Navy,' said Joe.

An odd result of this well-published incident was that the Ford Classic attracted larger than usual crowds. It is a sad reflection on modern sport that Muffin, and her antics, can attract spectators and greater media coverage than quieter and more successful players.

FAMOUS LAST WORDS

Perhaps the final thoughts on US professional golf should come from two great players.

'When men score badly, the weather is bad or the course is badly prepared. When women score badly it's because they're lousy golfers.'
(CAROL MANN, 1965 US Women's Open Champion)

'I can't see what is so terrible about being a professional. Amateurs and professionals both spend most of their lives on the golf course – the only difference is that the professional usually manages to keep his sense of humour.'
(GLENNA COLLETT VARE)

2 Following the Golf Stream

|P|erhaps it is typical of the American national characteristics, but the early US ladies' professional circuits seemed to be upfront, commercially backed attempts to change the world. Above all the British hate change and commercialism, and in the case of ladies' professional golf, the world had changed before they even realised the difference.

The British may have given golf to the world, but until the 1970s 'professionalism in golf' meant something totally different to British players than it meant to players like Babe Zaharias or Betsy Rawls.

KNOWING YOUR PLACE

In Britain the Victorian amateur golfer approved of the professional fraternity only because they knew their place. There were no problems with the tiny number of professional ladies, because they simply did not enter ladies' amateur competitions.

However within the ranks of gentlewomen amateurs a problem arose because of the new fashion for writing golf books and accepting money from publishers. Issette and her collaborators had produced *Our Lady of the Green*; May Hezlet wrote *Ladies Golf* and both LGU Assistant Secretary Mabel Stringer and Dorothy Campbell wrote professionally about golf.

The bending of the laws governing amateurism was not forced into the open by Issette, which was somewhat surprising given her 'angry buffalo' style of diplomacy. It was only after she retired that the LGU began to clamp down on the literary giants in its midst.

DON'T GIVE UP YOUR DAY JOB

During the mid-1920s, two of the biggest names in the sport came under investigation. Cecil Leitch severed her long standing links with the LGU when they started asking questions about her golf books. Joyce Wethered had also written several books, but managed to keep her amateur status.

Joyce's qualifications were especially shaky when she became manageress of the golf department of Fortnum and Masons' store in London and was still classed as an amateur. Triple British Champion Enid Wilson was deemed to

92

be a professional for doing a similar job in the golf department of Lillywhites.

Speaking 55 years later, Enid Wilson maintains that her only crime was to inform the English selectors that she was no longer available for international matches. This caused the amateur door to be slammed shut. Ironically, Enid later became ladies' amateur golf correspondent for *The Daily Telegraph* and the most famous ladies' golf writer of her era.

In 1935, some people were so upset at Enid's exclusion from the amateur ranks, that a move was made to allow professionals to play in the British Ladies' Championship. This would not have brought a flood of hardened professionals into that competition, for besides Enid and Joyce Wethered (who took professional status to play in America), there were only two or three other girls who could be classed as professionals. They worked in the pros shops run by their husband or boyfriend. To play in competition, these girls would have had to compete against men in open events. This was at a time when most of the men were barely able to make a living from the game. With limited opportunities, few ladies took the professional plunge and it was 1952 before the issue resurfaced, with the questionable treatment of Wanda Morgan and Jean Donald.

SHODDY WORK

In 1938, Dunlop offered British champion Wanda Morgan a job as a representative. Her task was to promote their company at competitions where most of her clients would be friends and former competitors. Scotland's Jean Donald later took on the same task for Penfold. The LGU said they were allowed to give unpaid 'clinics' promoted by their employers, but on no account were they to give paid lessons. For this concession, Jean and Wanda were classified as 'non-amateurs' rather than professionals. However, when they ceased working for their respective employers, they applied for and got back their full amateur status.

The issue seemed closed until Jean Donald was chosen for the 1952 Curtis Cup at Muirfield. The US team objected to her selection and an enquiry was held. As a result, both Jean and Wanda were promptly re-classified as professionals!

A party of American lady professionals including Babe Zaharias and Patty Berg, had played a series of matches in 1950 against Britain's top amateur girls (and a party of Walker Cup golfers whom they trounced). The visitors were treated royally, and it seemed that it was perfectly in order to be a lady professional – as long as you were from America.

BRITISH HOPEFULS

By the 1960s, the success of the US LPGA circuit had started to attract a tiny number of British girls. The most successful of them was Michelle (Mickey) Walker, a tall friendly girl from Yorkshire, who won the 1973 Trans-Mississippi Tournament. This was the first major win by a British girl in America since Pam Barton's US National win forty years earlier.

Another top player to try the US circuit was Vivien Saunders, a strong-willed, solidly built woman of medium height who combined top golf with degrees in psychology and business studies. The rigours of the US tour were too much for Miss Saunders, but she saw much to admire and on her return to Europe she was instrumental in the formation of the Women's Professional Golf Association in 1976.

DEAR MISS SAUNDERS, THANK YOU FOR APPLYING BUT . . .

Vivien Saunders had been an outstanding player, but it was her roles as coach, administrator, and opponent to the men's established control of the game that have singled her out in golfing history.

After her return to Britain, Vivien applied for 26 vacant professionals' jobs. She failed at every one despite her outstanding qualifications as player and coach (she had been the first woman to graduate from the PGA School at Lilleshall). Incensed by what she regarded as blatant discrimination, she took Richmond Council to court alleging sexual discrimination. As Vivien subsequently qualified as a solicitor, the local authority had a fight on their hands.

Another opponent was Royal St George's GC, who had never had a lady member and certainly not a woman professional. When St George's advertised for a professional, Vivien's name was amongst the applicants – but not surprisingly she was not given the position.

Despairing of all the male opposition, Vivien bought her own course in 1986 at Abbotsley, in Cambridgeshire. Here she operates a local and national coaching scheme supported by many ladies' county organisations. In 1987 her contribution to golf was recognised when Miss Saunders was selected as Sports Coach of the Year.

OPENING UP THE OPEN

One of Vivien's first acts on returning to Britain from the US Tour had been to boost the new British Women's Open Championship with £1000 of her own money. The climate seemed to be right for women's professional golf in Britain after the success of an annual European championship at Sunningdale, sponsored by Colgate-Palmolive and featuring a number of the major US girl golfers, with winners including Judy Rankin and Nancy Lopez.

Building on the Colgate competition, pop music promoter John Jones tried unsuccessfully to create a British LPGA. Vivien Saunders and former paint company executive, Barry Edwards, were more successful. They called a meeting at the Northampton offices of brewers Carlsberg to announce the formal creation of the WPGA Tour. Twelve top girl golfers attended. These included Mickey Walker, Jane Chapman, Cathy Panton, Christine Langford, Lesley Hush and Jane Forrest, with several more following.

Carlsberg's involvement was to promote a dozen tournaments all over Britain, with £200 guaranteed to the winner and prize money down to final place. The calendar was also boosted by several individual events such as the Lambert and Butler Matchplay and the £10,000 sponsored British Women's Open, run by the LGU.

Eventually 32 girls made up the tour, which was launched in 1979, and the whole proceedings had a team atmosphere. Life was extremely pleasant and even the least successful girls had no trouble paying their expenses.

SUPPORT FROM ABROAD

The new tour attracted some talented individuals. England's Jenny Lee Smith had worked hard to create a place for herself in the USA before injury had slowed her progress. Talented and experienced, Jenny found playing at home could be both profitable and enjoyable. And by a strange irony, she was joined by American girls, such as the former Curtis Cup player Peggy Conley who opted for the European game in preference to the US circuit.

A BLOW TO THE TOUR

Despite the influx of players, and a steady increase in sponsorship, the new organisation soon ran into problems. Barry Edwards stepped down, and even the legal title to the name of 'WPGA' became a matter of litigation. Eventually the WPGA separated from the men's PGA and became the Women's Professional Golf European Tour.

Another blow came when television coverage of the 1984 British Women's Open went horribly wrong. To fit in with other commitments, and to attract the premier American players, the British Women's Open was put back to October to be televised live, but the autumn of 1984 saw gales and rain ruining months of planning and hard work. In the teeth of freezing winds, players donned their winter woollies and struggled round the course in terrible conditions. Scoring was high as the conditions deteriorated, and the women's golf suffered, the result being that television companies wrote off ladies' golf as 'unpopular'.

Vivien Saunders, who overcame much prejudice to prove herself as a great player and coach

GIRLS ABROAD

The attitude to ladies' golf was somewhat different when a party of British girls was invited to take part in an important Pro-Am competition in Switzerland. There they were able to mix with some of the greatest names in the men's game.

Following this, even countries such as Belgium, Italy, France and Sweden invited the tour to their shores. In contrast to back home, the clubs in these countries thought it a great honour to entertain the cream of ladies' golf, to such an extent that club members opened their homes to the visitors. With support from foreign sponsors, tournaments were launched all over Europe

The sky's the limit for Britain's favourite golfing girl, Laura Davies

Previous page: *Trish Johnson won her first competition at twelve and subsequently became the first British girl to gain maximum points in a Curtis Cup match*

Above: *One of the most pleasant people in golf, Mickey Walker was an amateur champion before turning professional and becoming the first British girl for a generation to win a major event in America*

Right: *Amy Alcott began by destroying her dad's lawn. Today she destroys the competition*

Opposite: *Patty Sheehan. Tiny by golf standards, Patty has won two LPGA Championships – the second by 10 strokes*

Right: *The youngest player in Curtis Cup history, Vicki Goetze (USA) proved a brilliant golfer despite her seventeen years of age*

Below: *Helen Alfredsson is the latest of a string of top-class Swedish girls to grace the women's professional tour in Europe*

Opposite: *Laura Davies brought America to its knees by winning a play-off for the 1987 US Women's Open*

Following page: *Florence Descampe – the best ever Belgian girl golfer, who has emerged as a potential European professional champion*

Opposite: *Betsy King, one of only four golfers to win successive US Women's Opens*

Left: *Muffin Spencer-Devlin. Muffin packs in the spectators with her antics, but must wish she could also pack in her troubles*

Below: *Tall and willowy Beth Daniel is women's golf's biggest hitter and possibly its most outstanding modern player*

where the best of facilities and accommodation was laid on for the competitors. Things did occasionally go awry. The members of the tour were booked into 'chalets' at one resort, when summer had long gone. The chalets turned out to be bicycle sheds. The apologetic hosts soon rectified matters.

No such problems occurred in Belgium, where the local tournament has become one of their premier sporting events attracting vast numbers of spectators. Their own champion, Florence Descampe, has already reached celebrity status at home and in France, Marie Laure de Lorenzi has become a national heroine. The success of these girls has encouraged new players from virtually every European country.

Foreign girls starting on the tour are subsidised by sponsorship and have few financial worries. However, up and coming British girls now find sponsors hard to find, especially as the sponsors are aware of the lack of interest in the women's game by the British television companies.

Only the success of the WPG's most charismatic figure, Laura Davies, has brought any interest from the BBC or ITV.

LAURA DAVIES

If the average Briton was asked to name a lady golfer, most would probably nominate Laura Davies, from West Byfleet in Surrey, whose fearless attacking style brought her the British Open and US Open titles in consecutive years.

For someone who has become a great professional champion, Laura was not an outstanding amateur player. She did not begin to play golf until the relatively late age of fifteen, when she used to caddy for her brothers. Today, brother Tony caddies for Laura. Laura eventually became South East and English Intermediate Champion and a Curtis Cup player, but her early ventures were limited by a shortage of cash. The members of West Byfleet once had a whip-round to raise £100 to send her to the British Open.

The long-hitting girl turned professional in 1985 and shot straight to the top winning the 1986 British Ladies' Open and finishing No 1 tour player in 1985 and 1986. It is easy to assume that Laura anticipated instant success, but she took a huge gamble when she joined the WPG European Tour. She admits, 'I borrowed £1000 off my mum. I always knew that if I never looked like establishing myself I would quit, rather than keep missing the cut.'

The gamble paid off and in 1987 Laura took another risk. She tried her fortunes in America. Things did not start too well, but for her fourth American event she tackled the US Women's Open. She surprised herself by tieing for first place with JoAnne Carner and Ayako Okamoto. Laura said that she was totally relaxed before the play-off because nobody gave her an earthly chance against the two more famous names. Fortunately Laura also proved to have a superb short game and won the play-off to take the title and $55,000 in prize money. Her victory led the Tour to amend its constitution and grant her automatic LPGA membership.

In the next two seasons, she had success in Japan, America and Europe, but 1990 proved a relative disappointment. Although winning a tournament in Europe, her form at home and abroad slumped and she had problems with sponsorship. But Laura will not blame anyone except herself, saying, 'I don't worry. If I play badly, my game tends to sort itself out.' And in 1991 she was back on the winning trail for her fourth tournament success in America.

BIG AL

Alison Nicholas, the girl who replaced Laura Davies as British Women's Open Champion, has not received anything like the attention given to the West Byfleet girl.

Despite being the smallest girl in world class golf, 'Big Al', as she has become known, has established herself as an outstanding competitor with the priceless and enviable gift of total concentration on the course.

Alison, from Sheffield, was introduced to golf by her father, who improved her game to scratch in three years. After winning everything that northern golf had to offer, she won the 1983 British Strokeplay Championship before turning professional.

At first she gained a reputation as being a steady player, but then her career was set alight by a superb season in 1987, when she won the British Open and was voted 'most improved player'. Since then she has established herself amongst the best of Europe, with nine wins on tour.

Alison Nicholas – the smallest girl in world golf and potentially its biggest talent

SUCCESSES AND PROBLEMS

There has always been great interest in Ladies' professional golf, even in the Carlsberg days, but improvements in the playing standards have made even the men take notice (Dale Reid's win in the 1991 Ford Classic was a 21-stroke improvement on the 1982 winning score). The improvement has been fueled by an increase in new players which has in turn led to the introduction of 'cut-off' scores for tournaments. 'Missing the cut' is increasingly becoming a worry for new and struggling players for whom being well placed in an event has become a matter of economic necessity, rather than prestige.

The WPGET has also had its problems, especially with the US LPGA authorities who have severely limited the number of appearances LPGA players can make in Europe. In 1989 Jane Geddes risked a heavy fine when she decided to play in the British Open at Ferndown without a release from the LPGA – but she made sure she wouldn't be out of pocket by winning the title and first prize of £18,000! But her success has not led to a relaxation of their rules.

Antagonism was forgotten in December 1990 however, when a piece of golfing history was made. The first ever Solheim Cup, instituted on the lines of the men's Ryder Cup, brought together the finest American and European professional ladies at Lake Nona, Florida. America won 11½ – 4½ to confirm that they were still one shot ahead of their European cousins.

Part Three

1 Ladies' Golf Around the World

The first one hundred years of ladies' golf was dominated by Britain and the United States because so many of the early important decisions were made in those two countries.

But ladies' golf is now played in more than one hundred different countries. Simply because the game was shaped within two corners of the globe, it would be a mistake to ignore the wider world and thereby omit a large and colourful part of the sport. It is full of talented players and there are subtle shades of difference to what has gone before.

It would also be wrong to underestimate Scotland's part as the progenitor of world golf. We know that the Scots started the game in England and America, but what about the rest of the world? In answer to this, it has been found that Scottish folk figured prominently wherever golf is played: in the other home countries, Australia, New Zealand, Canada, Europe or Africa.

In many countries the early days of ladies' golf were a struggle. The women had to contend with their male counterparts' negative attitudes and therefore, very little assistance. After the emphasis shifted to England in 1893, the ladies' game in Scotland did not curl up and die; on the contrary it thrived.

We should therefore return to the misty linkslands along the Firth of Forth, and continue the story of the lady golfers of Bonnie Scotland.

Scotland

After Musselburgh's competition for the fishwives in 1810, references to ladies playing golf in Scotland are rare until the final part of the century. Instead there is the illusion of hard-hearted men in their vast palatial clubhouses, condemning their womenfolk to draughty old shacks where they sat round an open fire stoking the embers with their putters.

In 1860, the East Lothian Golf Club welcomed women – strictly for afternoon tea. Their status had barely risen by 1877, when the newly opened St Andrews ladies' course was described by a contemporary commentator as being 'unfit for rabbits'.

Emancipation almost arrived in 1890 at Lanark GC, where women were accepted as members. The committee donated an old shed behind the club-house as the ladies' room. Encouraged by such generosity the Lanark ladies asked the men's committee to allow a match against Wishaw Ladies on a Saturday afternoon. The men said 'Yes, but don't ask again.' They then told the ladies to remember their status as merely 'members of their own room' – or shed.

If the Lanark men seemed ungenerous, it should not be forgotten that at the time, women were banned from most Scottish clubs on Saturday afternoons, evenings and on competition days. Courses were also closed on Sundays.

ENTER MISS GRAINGER'S BOSOM

As the ladies were treated so badly, by 1902 Scottish ladies' golf was at a low ebb. The best players could make no impact at the highest level and those with talent were woefully ignorant of the rules. Miss Agnes Grainger of the St Rule Club, St Andrews, decided that something had to be done and she organised the Scottish Ladies' Golf Association to promote top-class competitions north of the border. Miss Grainger was something of a celebrity in the 'old grey toon' and is commemorated by a bunker on the main course named 'Miss Grainger's Bosom'. (History, unfortunately, does not tell us how the course designer went about checking the accuracy of his specifications.)

The first SLGA Championship was held at St Andrews in 1903 with Old Tom Morris as starter. Miss Grainger's fears about the naivety of the Scots lassies were justified when in the final, Alice Glover of Elie tried to flatten a hump on the green that stood in the way of a putt. The horrified officials had no option but to penalise Miss Glover, but this did not stop her beating Hoylake's Molly Graham.

Molly gained revenge the following year, but gave up entering the event when the great Dorothy Campbell proved too strong for allcomers and became the first great champion to use the SLGA Title as the springboard to greater glory.

STAYING THE COURSE

After Dorothy Campbell packed her clubs and headed for America, Charlotte Beddows (Watson) emerged to rank amongst the most remarkable golfers of the 20th century. Mrs Beddows represented Scotland for half a century until 1951 when she finally retired from the international stage at the age of 73; she continued to play for East Lothian for a further decade and is reported to have said, 'Unless I retire soon, I'll need a bath-chair not a golf trolley.'

Charlotte was the first of many great Scots girls to grace the Curtis Cup competition and eventually she lost her place to two girls whose brilliance is legendary: Helen Holm and Jessie Valentine (Anderson).

Mrs Holm (1909 – 1971) ended Scotland's 22-year spell without a British Champion when she defeated Pam Barton at Royal Porthcawl. She was exceptionally tall and possessed a slow, graceful swing that was given extra propulsion by moving on to her toes at impact.

WEE JESSIE

Helen Holm was unlucky to be a contemporary of Jessie Anderson, from Perth, one of the greatest Scots lady golfers of all time. The daughter of a professional, Jessie received her first club at the age of five and began a remarkable story of golfing success: British Girls' title, six Scottish Championships, three British Championships and seven Curtis Cup appearances.

From a well-known golfing family who have been associated with the game for generations, Jessie claimed major overseas titles – those of New Zealand and France – before gaining major success at home. She won the British title for the first time in 1937, but it was not until 1938 that she won her first Scottish Championship.

In 1958, a quarter of a century after winning the British Girls' title, Mrs

ABOVE LEFT The 19th century champion Old Tom Morris proved a useful ally to Agnes Grainger and the Scottish Ladies' Golf Association. He acted as starter for their early championships

ABOVE Helen Holm, who became the first British champion from north of the border for a generation when she won at Royal Porthcawl

Valentine won her third British title and played in her final Curtis Cup match in America where she helped retain the trophy. The match was tied after Great Britain and Ireland had won at Prince's Golf Club two years previously. She retired from competitive golf and took over her father's sports business and designed her own clubs, turning professional as a result.

She may have been small in stature, but with a club in her hand, Jessie possessed great style and grace. An opponent says of her that few players – men or women – in the history of the game, have had such command of every club in the golf bag. This was a legacy of natural athletic ability and her father's gentle but firm tuition.

In 1958 Jessie retired from competitive golf and was awarded the MBE for her services to sport – the first woman golfer to receive such recognition. Essentially a homebird, she admits her greatest happiness is living in her beloved Perthshire and playing golf at lovely Blairgowrie. When the British Stroke Play Championship was played there in 1986, she was in action again – caddying for the winner, Claire Hourihane, of Ireland!

Another great Scots girl golfer was Jean Donald (later Mrs Anderson) who made a huge impact as an unknown in 1947 by winning the French and Scottish titles. She then established herself as the best girl golfer in Europe by reaching the British Ladies' final at Royal Lytham and St Annes the following year, at the age of 17.

After surviving the brambles and bracken of the famous links, Jean walked on to the 18th green knowing that two putts would tie America's Louise Suggs. The retired colonels and tired businessmen on the terrace put down their gins and prepared to applaud the Scots girl, but they turned away in anguish as the second putt failed to drop. The whoops of joy from the American contingent only added to Miss Donald's loneliness.

Like Mrs Valentine, she also was classed as professional when she became involved in designing golf equipment. She devoted much time to giving golf clinics, mainly at junior championships.

PLENTY TO SMILE ABOUT ON MONDAY MORNING

Since the days when Jean and Jessie were classed as professionals, the desirability of joining the paid ranks has increased and several Scots girls have become top-class performers on the European tour.

Amongst the first was Cathy Panton, daughter of the famous Scots professional, John Panton. Cathy was British Champion in 1976 when the championship, and Cecil Leitch, returned to the famous old links at Silloth. Receiving trophies was commonplace to Cathy, before she became a founder member of the Women Professional Golfers European Tour. She continued the habit on the professional circuit, claiming 14 victories between 1979 and 1988.

Gillian Stewart from Inverness was another early supporter of the professional tour, but only as an amateur. Her life changed when she won the 1984

Jessie Anderson (Valentine) MBE – a great and enduring talent

European Open and was not eligible for the prize money. The next year she turned professional and won the Ford Ladies Classic twice and the prize money that went with it!

Dale Reid of Ladybank GC had also had plenty to smile about after 20 tour wins and twice topping the Order of Merit.

LOCAL HEROINES

When the European season is over, many of Scotland's top girl golfers return to their home clubs and can be seen playing over the links with other members. Jane Connachan can still be found in the winter months at Royal Musselburgh. The Scots take more pride in their best girl golfers (amateur or professional) than any other nationality.

Any portrait of the great modern golfers must also mention an amateur who has become one of Scotland's greatest sporting heroines.

BELLE OF THE GOLF BALL

Belle Robertson, MBE, comes from the long tradition of Dorothy Campbell and Jessie Anderson – talent combined with stamina to remain at the top.

A farmer's daughter from Dunaverty on the West Coast, the talent of Belle McCorkindale almost went unnoticed, until the club's caddymaster recommended the 20 year old to the area's premier club, Machrihanish, as a player of outstanding potential who could outhit the best men.

'I was never an elegant type of player with a slow, stylish swing and had no great natural advantages, being only of average height. My long-hitting from the tee came because working on a farm makes you fit and strong,' says Belle (Mrs Robertson).

Machrihanish polished up the gem and at 25 she was West of Scotland Champion and went on to win seven Scottish Championships. Modestly she says that her first Curtis Cup appearance came because other girls were unavailable. However, one of America's greatest amateurs, Anne Sander, nominates Belle as an outstanding post-war British player with a tremendous competitive instinct. Belle eventually won seven Curtis Cup caps and twice was non-playing captain.

'Having come late into the game, in later years I tried stepping down and becoming a spectator,' says Belle. 'But I'd win something else and the whole playing side would restart. That was how it was. I never intended to carry on until my forties or fifties.'

'Having won the British Stroke Play title for the third time the high spot of Belle's career came with the 1981 British Amateur Championship at Conwy when she reached her fourth final. She already had three runner-up medals for this competition and therefore felt that her chances of winning seemed to be ebbing away. After meeting a string of top-class players in the qualifying rounds, she faced fellow Scot, Wilma Aitken, in the final.

The final was going the way the uncommitted wanted. Belle was 5 up with

Dale Reid – one of a number of outstandingly talented Scots professionals

Belle Robertson, whom the Americans consider the toughest British competitor of modern times

5 to play when disaster struck. Her wayward drive at the 13th hit a spectator. Belle's concentration was affected by the ensuing delay and Wilma won the next five holes.

While the final was an all Scots affair, the Welsh crowd were delighted as Belle recovered to win the second extra hole and the title she wanted most. A fitting – and triumphant – farewell to a great international career came when at the age of 50 – the oldest player to compete in the matches – she played a vital part in Kansas in 1986 in a momentous Curtis Cup victory, the first on American soil.

Wales

Although the Scots played an important part in founding Welsh golf by working as professionals and course designers, their influence was less than in the other home countries because the early Welsh courses were established by wealthy local businessman. Their aim was to copy the game's success in England and Scotland. So much the better if the golf could attract holidaymakers to small seaside towns such as Tenby and Porthcawl, where the attractions were a beach, a bel vista, and plenty of open space for the new game.

Tenby was the first Welsh golf course to open in 1888. Soon afterwards, a large number of courses began opening on the north and south coasts of the Principality. Wales's major golfing problem had already emerged. Courses on the flat green coastal margins could support themselves from the local population and from holidaymakers (24 of Conwy's first 28 lady members lived in England). However, the rural areas had few potential golfers and even fewer visitors. Consequently only a small number of courses opened in Mid-Wales and they were often built on barren ragged hillside. Mid-Wales still has fewer courses than anywhere elsewhere in mainland Britain.

The course building boom of the 1890s gave Mid-Wales several superb parkland courses, notably at Aberdovey. This was the venue of the 1901 British Ladies' Open and, encouraged by the championship, the Welsh Ladies' Golf Union was formed in 1904 and their first Welsh Close Championship was held in 1905.

Little is known about the first winner, Miss E Young, but 1906 saw the emergence of the Duncan girls from Penarth GC who were prominent in Welsh golf for the next 20 years. Blanche Duncan (1879 – 1927) was champion five times, and her sister-in-law Marjorie Duncan (1890 – 1967) was champion three times in the 1920s, first winner of the Glamorgan Championship and she played for the county on 136 occasions.

NOTHING FURTHER COULD BE DESIRED

The top British players returned to the Principality in 1926 when Cecil Leitch took her fourth British title at Royal St David's in the shadow of Harlech Castle. But for players of a lower order, life could be fairly primitive.

On one occasion, Royal Porthcawl Ladies complained to the club about the head greenkeeper's gruesome habit of putting rabbit traps in the bunkers. The committee tried to smooth ruffled feelings by providing a bathhouse, and electricity for the ladies' rooms. A note of thanks records 'Now that electric light has been installed, nothing further could be desired.'

Blanche Duncan captained Glamorgan to the 1909 Welsh Championship win. Blanche herself also won five Welsh titles

HOW MANY GREENS HAS MY VALLEY

The ladies were therefore able to sit in their baths and read the bestselling book of the era *How Green was my Valley*, which told of a doctor's life in South Wales. The story had echoes in Welsh golf when smallpox inter-

Mrs Marjorie Duncan takes the Welsh Ladies' title at Royal St David's, Harlech

rupted county matches which had never been merged into a separate Welsh Division. (The counties of Wales always opted to play their English neighbours rather than travel to the other end of the Principality.)

Arrangements were thrown into disarray in 1931, when Devon and Cornwall refused to visit Glamorgan and Monmouth after an outbreak of smallpox in Newport. Eventually the problem was solved. An official was placed at a table, outside the clubhouse, and insisted that caddies and players had to produce certificates of vaccination, as well as handicap certificates, before being admitted.

DROPPING OFF THE VAN

Other ladies who had problems with official documentation were Mrs Rieben and her daughter Isabel.

The mother was Welsh Champion in 1929 and 1936 but her real name was

Mrs Van Rieben. Her German-born husband had scandalised polite society by abandoning his wife and young baby to fight for the Kaiser in the First World War. Perhaps wisely, for his wife was a large, strongly built woman, Herr Van Rieben never returned to Aberdovey and the abandoned wife raised Isabel alone.

Isabel emulated her mother's Welsh Championship success in 1932 and 1934 under her maiden name. She won again in 1948 as Mrs Seely and for a fourth time in 1951 as Mrs Bromley-Davenport.

After Isabel Bromley-Davenport, a number of outstanding Welsh girl golfers emerged, notably Susan Bryan-Smith, Ruth Ferguson, Marjorie Barron and Nancy Cook.

After these girls came Pat Roberts, who won four Welsh titles and despite holding office in Welsh ladies' golf, she found time to win Newport's club championship on 25 consecutive occasions and the county title 18 times.

Two fine Welsh champions – Mrs Marjorie Duncan and Mrs Rieben. Mrs Duncan took the honours

CURTIS CUP CONNECTIONS

The best Welsh girl golfer never to win a national title was Elsie Brown of Maesdu who was runner-up 5 times. However, she had the honour of being the first girl selected for Curtis Cup duty.

As reserve, Elsie had to wait by the telephone without getting summoned but it rang for Tegwen Perkins (Thomas) of Pennard who was called up as a surprise late replacement for the Curtis Cup in 1974. In the 1976 Curtis Cup at Royal Lytham she took 3 points of 4.

Tegwen's biggest rival came from her own club of Pennard, near Swansea, in Vicki Thomas, one of the three golfing sisters from Bargoed. The cheerful effervescent Vicky won the Welsh Championship for a record seventh time in 1991 and lost another final to her sister Kerry. She also won the Welsh Open Stroke Play title for the third time in 1989, two years after becoming New Zealand Stroke Play Champion.

Vicki went on to become one of the best British players of the 1980s and into the 90's, competing in five Curtis Cup teams including the victorious teams of 1986 and 1988 (with Elsie Brown as vice-captain).

WELCOME VISITOR

The upturn in Welsh fortunes in the 1970s coincided with the introduction of the new Welsh Open Stroke Play Championship, which attracted many of the best British girls, notably the teenage Laura Davies and local girl Trish Johnson.

Trish began playing golf at Royal North Devon as a child with her three brothers and developed from them a most unladylike ability to hit the ball an enormous distance. With Westward Ho!'s reeds and shallow ditches, it is not guaranteed that you'll find the ball where you expect it.

Young Miss Johnson coped well enough and found herself, at twelve years of age, winning her first competition as a 33-handicapper which had shrunk to plus 1 when her father's change of job led the family to cross the Bristol Channel. Despite a three-year qualification period for Wales, she was eligible for the 1986 Curtis Cup where she became the first British player ever to take a maximum four points.

The professional tour beckoned in 1987 and three wins as a rookie could not equal the joy of coming top of the American LPGA Qualifying School in Texas, by six clear strokes. But despite the lure of America, she has not deserted the WPG European Tour, winning the Order of Merit in 1990.

INTERNATIONAL TIES

Even with the services of Trish Johnson, Vicki Thomas and, in a bygone age, the Duncan girls, the Welsh International team has always had a struggle to compete with their neighbours, who have so many more players to choose from.

Although Wales began competing in the four-nations Home Champion-ship in 1909, it was 13 years before the first win came. This was against Ireland and because both Celtic nations lack the population to consistently mount major challenges at international level, a close relationship has developed between the two countries for Ireland, like Wales, has a colourful golfing history.

The 1988 Curtis Cup. Vicki Thomas drives at Royal St George's, partnering Jill Thornhill to a handsome win in the foursomes

Ireland

The game of golf crossed the Irish Sea with the early Scots' settlement of Ulster in the 17th century. It had therefore been played in Ulster for many years before 1850, when Scottish army units established a course on the Curragh, near Dublin. When the Scottish army moved off to India, they took the game with them and it was 1881 before the first permanent golf course was established at Holywood on the shore at Belfast Lough in Northern Ireland.

Seven years later the first seeds of ladies' golf were planted in Ireland with the opening of a nine-hole course at the tiny Ulster port of Portrush. Visitors alighted here from Glasgow, and the first ladies' club was opened at Holywood (thereby preceding similar ventures at Killymoon, Buncrana and at beautiful Royal County Down).

Encouraged by this interest, a meeting was called in Belfast in 1893 and the Irish LGU was formed, with a local girl Clara Mulligan as its first secretary and national champion.

ENGLISH MISSIONARIES AND IRISH TROUBLES

Miss Mulligan persuaded the Ladies' Golf Union to hold their third Championship at Portrush in 1895. This venture helped Royal Portrush to recruit 290 local ladies as members, including two youngsters May Hezlet and Rhoda Adair who later became British champions.

The decline of Hezlet and Adair coincided with Ireland's descent into the 'Troubles' which caused disruption in all areas of Irish life. In 1920 terrorists mistook Douglas Golf Club for the home of a local dignitary and they burnt down the clubhouse by mistake. But as many of the old clubhouses had a remarkable tendency to disappear in flames, the terrorists were probably pre-empting the inevitable.

The split into Ulster and the Irish Free State came in 1921. Even so, on both sides of the border, there will always be lovely people with their own delightful approach to life. In particular, at Malahide GC, one of the vaguest and perhaps all-embracing golf rules ever to be introduced, was brought to their players' attention in 1925. It simply said that 'Any non congenial of either sex will have his or her ticket revoked.'

LOOKING INWARD

With the division of Ireland, it was not surprising that Irish golf went through a period of introspection between the wars. Top Irish players fell way behind their counterparts on the mainland. Mrs J Jackson was the outstanding golfer, winning six Irish Close titles.

Another outstanding and durable competitor was Dorothy Pim who took up golf after an illustrious career as a hockey international. Under her married name of Mrs Beck she became Curtis Cup Captain and the subject of a remarkable newspaper misprint in 1946.

Douglas Caird of *Fairway and Hazard* magazine wrote an editorial that read, 'And so, to Mrs Beck and the Curtis Cup Team we wish good luck.' It appeared in print as 'And sod Mrs Beck and the Curtis Cup Team'. She enjoyed the joke and settled out of court for six copies to show her friends.

OUTWARD SIGNS

Better times for Irish golf were signalled by the emergence of the first Irish girl for a generation to travel abroad and win honours. She was Pat Walker of Malahide who was three times selected for the Curtis Cup, and won the 1935 Australian Ladies' Championship.

Another noted globe-trotter was Clarrie Tiernan of the County Louth

GC, Drogheda, who won the 1936 Irish title and was invited to America. There she was runner-up in the Canadian Championship at Royal Ottawa, and winner of the New Jersey Open.

Clarrie was a fine golfer whose career was approaching its peak when the Second World War brought an end to competitive golf, even in the neutral Irish republic. When golf was resumed after the war, an even finer golfing champion emerged, Philomena Garvey.

GROWING UP ON THE LINKS

The lush green links of County Louth GC in Drogheda were a heaven-sent playground for the local children who, when the course was quiet, had the space and scenery to provide a stage for any youthful dream. Just to one side of the famous course was the Garvey's house. The children grew up in this magical setting and when they were tired of playing cowboys and bandits, they began to imitate the local golfers.

One brother became the local golfing champion, but it was daughter Philomena Garvey who put Ireland's name into golfing history. Tall and erect she was chosen for the 1948 Curtis Cup match on the strength of three Irish Ladies' title victories. Thus began a long and distinguished association with the event. 'I was picked for the Curtis Cup team on seven occasions. You cannot say that any particular match was more memorable than the rest, simply because being selected was always something special, no matter how many times it had happened before.'

Philomena is keen to clear up one misunderstanding that has developed over her Curtis Cup association. It is said that the team was renamed 'Great Britain and Ireland' after her protests that the name of 'Great Britain' was unfair to her home country. 'That is not correct,' she says. 'The team name had always been Great Britain and Ireland, but probably due to lack of space on the official badge, the Irish part had been omitted. I simply pointed this out to the organisers who were happy to correct the omission.'

Besides her Curtis Cup record, Philomena won every honour the game can bestow. She is closely associated with the British Championship where she made five appearances in the final and won in 1957. 'The highspot of my career,' she says. And her record in the Irish Ladies' Championship is peerless: 15 finals, 15 wins.

In 1965 Philomena became Ireland's first professional, but much confusion has surrounded her decision. 'In 1950, I had played against the US women professionals and I only just lost to Babe Zaharias. Her manager (Fred Corcoran) asked me to turn professional and move to America. I didn't really fancy living out of a suitcase and have been happy to stay in Ireland. I worked in a sports shop for a number of years and never had a problem with the R & A over my amateur status.

Later, in 1965, I turned professional purely because I wanted to give lessons, but I gave that up eventually and had to serve a two-year qualifying period before winning my fifteenth Irish Championship in 1970.'

STRIKING LUCKY

Besides Miss Garvey, other Irish girls have performed well in the Curtis Cup, notably Zara Bolton of Royal Portrush, who is Irish by adoption having married a local doctor. Legend has it that the couple first met when Zara's wayward tee shot struck Dr Bolton's car during the 1939 British Ladies' Open.

Mrs Bolton played in the 1948 Curtis Cup match, but will be best remembered for captaining the victorious 1956 team, and for the radical departure of taking the British team to Portrush for a week's practice before the competition, where they played the best local men players.

Another Curtis Cup heroine was the slightly built Kitty McCann who was twice national champion and who played in the winning Great Britain and Ireland team at Muirfield in 1952. A prolific winner of Irish provincial titles, Kitty's career was cut short by back trouble.

In recent times Mary McKenna, of Donabate GC, Dublin, has come closest to emulating Philomena Garvey's achievements. She has won the Irish title eight times and, with nine appearances, has been a stalwart of the Curtis Cup team from the darkest days to the finest hours of 1986.

Ireland's major contributor to the professional ranks is Maureen Madill of Coleraine, Co Derry, the wife of Ryder Cup player and teacher John Garner. She won the British Stroke Play title in 1980 before turning professional in 1986.

A TOUCH OF THE BLARNEY

Ireland's relationship with mainland Britain is a complicated one. An Irish golfer once explained her nation's feeling about this relationship by quoting the story of Clarrie Tiernan, who achieved great things in America in 1938.

When early news of Clarrie's fine performance in the Canadian Open was telegraphed to London, a famous Fleet Street newspaper carried the headline 'BRITISH GIRL ON VERGE OF CANADIAN TRIUMPH!'

The next day she fell away and was second after the final round. The same newspaper had a tiny piece reading 'Irish Girl beaten.'

CELTIC TRADITIONS

Another country with Irish connections is Australia, but the Scots created the connection with the game of golf.

Australia – Green And Golf

The continent of Australia was discovered in 1776 by Captain James Cook, but a century earlier the Dutch explorer, Abel Tasman, had found its southern island which he modestly called Tasmania. Nobody seemed to care much for Tasmania because it was ignored until the 19th Century. Scottish settlers arrived then and inevitably there are reports of golf being played on courses that have long since disappeared.

Philomena Garvey – possibly the finest Irish lady golfer of all time

115

In 1827 two Scotsmen were seen playing golf on the island. Several years later Alexander Reid of Hobart built himself a small course at Ratho.

But if Tasmania gave the southern hemisphere its first taste of golf, it also provided the first example of discrimination 60 years later. A nurse, Florence Barnes of Launceston, started a small golf club in the local hospital grounds. The hospital doctors were so indignant that they formed their own club and specifically excluded Miss Barnes and any other female. Florence should then have moved to the mainland where golf had been slower to develop, but the treatment of lady golfers was far better.

ON THE MAINLAND

On the mainland, yet another Scot, James Ross, tried unsuccessfully to establish a club at Flagstaff Hill, Melbourne, in 1847. The sport failed to take root until the three Royal clubs of Australia were formed – Melbourne (1891), Adelaide (1892) and Sydney (1893).

Melbourne allowed women membership from its formation and another new club at Geelong formed a ladies' section in 1893. A friendly match between the ladies of the two clubs led to the foundation of the first Australian Ladies Championship in 1894 which was organised by the men's Australian Golf Union. The first champion was Miss C M Mackenzie, who scored 131 for 36 holes, over what must have been a very short course.

Ladies' golf flourished but the sheer size of the new country was always going to be a major drawback, not least because golfers faced immense difficulty in travelling to competitions. In an effort to save money, Interstate Matches (which at first only involved New South Wales, Victoria, South Australia and Tasmania), were played on the first day of the national championship.

The keenness of girls from all over Australia to support ladies' matches drew the admiration of the men, and in 1903 the country's foremost male golfer D G Soutar wrote:

'I am convinced that the majority of Australian women who follow golf like it, first and foremost, for the healthy open air exercise it affords. It promotes self-control which steadies the nerve. It takes women out of themselves, and acts as a gentle counterpoise to tea and gossip.'

Inspired by such patronising words, a group under Lady Halse Rogers started a ladies' golf union of their own. In 1920 it affiliated to the British LGU, and adopted Issette Pearson's handicapping system.

This move created considerable misgivings among some state organisations. They felt their own homespun rules were better suited to the local conditions. Miss Pearson of Wimbledon had, after all, never had to consider rules governing kangaroos bounding across the fairways, or large birds of prey eating golf balls; or that Brisbane GC would issue swimming costumes to caddies so that precious golf balls could be recovered from the local creek.

GREEN AND GOLD TIES

In 1926, the men felt that the ALGU were reasonably in control of ladies' golf and they passed over the Australian Ladies' Cup. Another major cup competition developed in 1933, when Australia played New Zealand in the biennial 'Tasman Cup'. This was consolation for the refusal of Great Britain to send a touring team down under.

Britain relented in 1935, and a team of youngsters, including Pam Barton, was sent for a three-month tour. The prodigious Miss Barton announced her presence by taking eight strokes off the ladies 18-hole course record at Royal Canberra.

Australia was not totally overawed by the visitors and they acquitted themselves well in the following matches played on the visit. The country was already producing some fine players, notably Mona McLeod and Joan Fisher.

WAR AND PEACE

The Second World War put an end to all organised competition but by its end, the world seemed a smaller place. Many Australian service personnel had travelled abroad, mainly to 'the old country', and had struck up friendships. These led to tours by Australian sporting teams which became a major feature of post-war Britain.

The ALGU also wanted to send a team to Britain, to repay the 1935 visit, and a tour fund was generously supported by the world famous singer Dame Joan Hammond. She had been three times New South Wales golf champion before she went to Europe for singing lessons. Her state's LGU had helped to pay for Joan's tuition in Europe and the great lady repaid her debt by organising four concerts which helped raise $20,000 – twice the sum required.

The visit to Great Britain was a great success and gave the visitors a chance to compete in the 1950 British Championship where the tall, long-hitting Joanne Percy reached the semi-finals. Another team member who earned much acclaim was Pat Borthwick who became the nation's best-known girl golfer.

Although the tour proved that a gulf existed between the two nations' playing standards, it hardly merited the LGU's pompous rebuke of 'not yet good enough' when Australia asked to join in the Curtis Cup.

FLYING GOLF DOCTORS

Closer to home, the 1950s saw the ALGU begin a series of intensive golf schools for their best players, but the size of Australia proved to be a big handicap. Some girls had to fly 4,000 miles to attend the week-long coaching session.

Attempts were also being made to establish closer links between clubs within the continent. This could only be done by ALGU officials flying hun-

Jan Stephenson, the top Australian player, who has brought more than a little colour to the game in recent years

dreds of miles into the outback by light aircraft. They often landed in remote hamlets whose only claim to fame was a rough nine-hole course. The host clubs were always thrilled at the visits and invariable 'killed the fatted calf' by laying on a huge meal and gallons of alcohol. By the end of a fortnight, the ALGU officials were glad to see civilisation again, 'So we don't have to face another decent meal.'

In the outback the development of golf even began to affect the kangaroos. They soon learnt that golfers often carried plentiful supplies of food. One crafty kangaroo in Shepparton, Victoria, made a career of bouncing on to the green when golfers appeared and refusing to leave until he was given something to eat – aah, well, golf has always had its fair share of freeloaders.

PACIFIC INFLUENCES

By the 1970s ladies' golf was changing with the success of the American LPGA Tour which led to the formation of the Ladies' Professional Golf Association of Australia. The professional game has become the aim of many of the best Australian girl golfers, and one particular girl from down under has become well known in America, often for the wrong reasons.

SNAPPERS AND KIDNAPPERS

Being snapped and kidnapped are amongst the 'highlights' of the incident-strewn career of Jan Stephenson, the blonde bombshell who is probably the best woman golfer produced by Australia.

The daughter of a Sydney bus mechanic, the juvenile Jan was so outstanding at golf, tennis and swimming she could have earned a living from any of the three. She opted for golf because her dad preferred watching it on television.

The only monotonous thing she ever did in her life was to keep entering, and winning, the NSW Girls' title from 12 to 18 years of age. At 15, she added the New South Wales and Australian Foursomes titles. She turned professional at 22, and rapidly became Australia's no 1 professional girl.

In 1974 Jan joined the LPGA Tour and was Rookie of the Year. By 1976 she was 11th on the LPGA list of moneywinners despite the back trouble which has intermittently dogged her career.

IN THE BUFF

Controversy has dogged her career as well, and she annoyed many of her LPGA colleagues with her flagrant use of her sex appeal to promote herself.

An unsavoury fashion had developed amongst the more sensational magazines for offering the world's most beautiful women huge sums of money to pose semi-naked. The offers went out to TV and film stars, entertainers and sports stars. Most rejected the overtures except Jan who ended up on Page 3. Fellow LPGA member Jane Blalock commented that Jan must have confused glamour with 'trash'.

Corinne Dibnah winning the 1988 British Open, one of many wins on the European Tour for the talented Australian girl

Jan defines her philosophy of life as doing her best in a tournament and then walking away, winner or loser. It's best to leave the next day's golf to itself.

KIDNAPPED BY HER HUSBAND

Sadly her private life has been difficult to walk away from, with three marriages ending in divorce, including the USA's most notorious wedding of the decade.

Managed at the time by Eddie Vossler (who she lived with) and Larry Kolb, Jan married Mr Kolb but rapidly decided she preferred Mr Vossler. Mr Kolb retaliated by trying to kidnap his wife. The marital problems spilt over on to the golf course when Mr Kolb tried to resolve matters halfway round an LPGA competition. Inevitably the law became involved, and an Alabama judge sent Jan off to a clinic to sort herself out. Undaunted, Jan bounced back to win the 1982 Women's Open and the 1983 LPGA Championship.

Despite the excitement Jan has won 16 US tour events worth $2 million. However, her career seemed over in 1989, after a Miami mugger broke her hand trying to steal her wedding ring. Ironically, the ring was given to her by her third husband who she had recently asked for a divorce.

COLD COMFORT

The other best-known Australian girl on the US tour is Jane Crafter, who qualified as a pharmacist before turning to golf full-time.

On the European professional tour, Australian girls Corinne Dibnah, winner of the 1988 British Open, Karen Lunn and Ann Jones have proved solid and reliable competitors. But Europe has never had the golden sunshine that Australia offers in such profusion and the Australian girls head for home when the European season is over. They tend to combine business with pleasure by then playing on the Far East Tour which culminates in the Australian Ladies' Open.

Not all Australian girls, however, seek professional glory. Outstanding amateurs of recent years have been Edwina Kennedy, who on her first visit, won the British Championship in 1978 at the age of 19, and went on to win the Canadian, New Zealand and Australian titles, and Louise Briers, runner-up in the British Championship, who has represented her country in every international event at home and overseas.

In the 1990s the marvellous climate of Australia has made it a successful tourist centre for sunseekers from the old world and ironically a new breed of Scots are visiting Australia to play golf over the magnificent new courses that are being constructed along the coasts that Captain Cook once explored.

The Scots Leave Their Marker – New Zealand, Canada, Africa

During the reign of Queen Victoria, a large portion of the globe was shaded red to show British influence. A similar map showing the spread of sport would have been shaded tartan, for the Scots spread the game of golf throughout the world.

Besides Australia, three other areas of British influence were opened up during the 19th Century by golfing pioneers: New Zealand, Canada and Africa.

New Zealand

Scots immigrants helped in much of the early development of New Zealand. They liked the islands, which so closely resembled parts of their homeland.

The first New Zealand golf club was formed in September, 1863, in the city of Dunedin which has always had a large number of Scots amongst its population. The club's order of balls and clubs from the homeland ran into a few problems. Parcel post was not up to modern standards, and it was six years before the equipment arrived in Dunedin. Eventually, the first recorded golf shot was played in 1869 by Charles R Howden who tried to keep the new course in business but problems with cattle and course maintenance proved insurmountable; a fate that befell a similar venture at Hagley Park, Christchurch, soon afterwards. Here, golfers decided it was better to be on the horns of a dilemma as to how to spend one's spare time – than on the horns of an aggressive bull!

Christchurch GC was revived in 1891 at Shirley, on the outskirts of the city. Ladies played a prominent part from the start; as they did at Otago GC where 24 ladies figured amongst the founder members.

In September, 1893, Otago Ladies organised a three-day championship and invited competitors from the other new clubs that were springing up all over the dominion. The first championship winner was Mrs Lomax-Smith of Christchurch.

The NZLGU historian, Mrs Val Cullen, records that early ladies' championships were certainly formal. 'It was customary for players to wear club uniform of a black Norfolk jacket and skirt, blouse and red tie.' The only way to tell players apart was by the ribbon in the club colours worn on their straw boater.

MEN AND FRIENDS

The men's golfing authorities governed all ladies' golfing matters until 1905, when eleven ladies' clubs broke away eventually to form the NZLGU. This affiliated to the British LGU after treasurer Blanche Hulton travelled down under and persuaded New Zealand's ladies to accept Issette Pearson's method of handicapping. The new organisation thrived and by 1919 had 7,500 members at 52 different clubs.

New Zealand's first great champion was Mrs Guy Williams of Auckland, who won five national championships and was one of the first New Zealand girls to travel abroad. She reached the semi-finals of the British and French championships. In 1920, she took the Australian Ladies' title, becoming the first player to win both of the Australasian titles.

Her great rival was Bonnie Templer who won three national titles but won no plaudits in 1914 for wearing a golfing skirt that clearly showed her ankles. The other outstanding local players of the era, who dressed more conventionally, were Bessie Gainsford, and Olive Fullerton-Smith who also won the Australian title.

Australian girls sought revenge by challenging for the New Zealand title. Finally, in 1933 the numbers of girls crossing the Tasman Sea justified a cup match between the two nations. Played at Victoria GC, Melbourne, the competition was christened 'The Tasman Cup'. New Zealand's team took the field (and the cup) at Melbourne. This was immediately after three days at sea and a night's rail journey.

NOT ALL BLACK

In 1935 the first British touring team played at Wellington in the championships. It resulted with a win for the great Scots champion Jessie Valentine. The British team cut such a sway through Australasia that a story emerged where one local golf official was asked,

'What was the best golf team ever to leave New Zealand or Australia?'

'The 1935 British team,' she replied. 'And damned glad we were to see the back of them – they won everything there was to play for.'

DECLINE AND RISE

After the Second World War, the standard of New Zealand golf fell behind the opposition and foreign visitors such as Australia's Maxine Bishop and the English champions Victoria Anstey and Julia Greenhalgh exported the national title.

The NZLGU fought back by establishing District Golf Associations. Their task was to upgrade the standards of local adult competition and they led the world by inaugurating national and district junior golf societies.

Within a decade, New Zealand was again producing champions, notably Marilyn J Smith who was top of the Australian moneywinners in 1973. She eventually moved to the US LPGA, and also collected many prizes on the burgeoning Japanese Tour during a long career. She paid her dues to New Zealand golf by touring the country and giving golf lectures and clinics. She also presented a New Zealand 'Golfer of the Year' award to be awarded each year.

Inspired by Marilyn Smith's example, a number of New Zealand girls have turned professional, notably Janice Arnold and Joanne Green.

Amongst the amateurs, the country has twice been second in the World

Amateur Championships (the Espirito Santo Cup) and Jan Higgins was second in the world rankings. Marnie McGuire at 17 became the youngest winner this century of the British Championship in 1986.

In recent times, a trend has developed for foreign players to compete in the New Zealand championship. Korean and Japanese ladies have become a regular feature. With players flying in from Tokyo just to play golf, it has all come a long way from poor Mr Howden, standing by his postbox for six years waiting for his clubs to arrive.

Canada

Canadian Golf began with a real mixed foursome in 1826, when there were reports of fur traders and bankers in Montreal, a city where Scots were an important part of the community and had their own 'St Andrews Society'.

By the time of the next reports of golf being played, the fur traders had departed leaving the 'fur-ways' to the banking fraternity. Eight bankers clubbed together and formed the 'City of Montreal GC'. They imported North America's first professional, W F Davis from Hoylake. Davis was not over-impressed with his new life, complaining bitterly that he had never had to work with a wheelbarrow back home.

AN INVITATION TO TEA

Women first came on the Canadian golfing scene in 1891, when Royal Montreal tried an experiment of allowing women into the clubhouse for tea. What the experiment was intended to prove is not known – presumably it was to show that any well-bred young lady who could hold a tea-cup, would also be as adept with a putter. Anyway, the experiment was a success and twenty ladies were allowed to join as playing members.

By 1901 dozens of other golf clubs had opened, and women players were sufficiently numerous for Royal Montreal to host the first Canadian Ladies' Championship which was won by the local member, Lillas Young. She was entitled to expect some official recognition of her achievement, but the club committee totally ignored her.

Less easy to ignore was the visit of 1903 World Champion, Rhoda Adair, who helped establish links with Britain that were further strengthened when Canada sent a team over to the British Championships. There they were honoured with a match against the host's second team known as 'the Rags'.

The trip was far from a disaster for Violet Pooley became the first foreigner to reach the British semi-finals and the visit encouraged Canada's ladies to form their own golf union.

GETTING PARTICULAR

The CLGU appointed one of its top players, Florence Harvey, as 'Hon Sec'. She encouraged the adoption of Issette Pearson's ideas on handicapping and

Marlene Stewart – the first Canadian world champion golfer

introduced 'Pars Committees' to assess the standard scratch score of the different ladies' courses. (20 years later the Canadian men's authorities adopted the same idea of 'Pars Committees').

Miss Harvey was an accomplished golfer, but she was some way behind the best Canadian lady of the era, Ada Mackenzie (1891 – 1973) who won five Open Championships and even founded her own club, strictly for lady golfers, in Toronto.

The only challenge to Ada for the honour of being the nation's best was Marlene Stewart (Streit). As a child in Ontario, she dominated junior golf before beginning a similar monopoly of the National Open and Close titles.

Until Marlene appeared, the principal Canadian Open competitions had been easy pickings for foreign girls, but Miss Stewart soon reversed the trend, winning the 1953 British title, the 1963 Australian Championship and the 1966 World Championship and, most precious of all, she became the first girl from north of the 49th parallel to win the US Amateur Title. With this single win, Canadian women's golf came of age.

Africa

Golf in Africa is principally the story of the sport in South Africa, for the first clubs were established in the union and a century later it has more

courses and golfers, of either sex, than the remainder of the continent. As ever, Scottish names figure everywhere but some of these pioneers carried a musket, whilst other chose a prayer book.

Amongst the musket carriers was General Sir Henry Torrens who founded the (Royal) Cape Town GC in 1885, the first club on the continent. It was however another twenty years before women began playing golf regularly on the urban courses of the union.

Elsewhere, the only golfers were Church of Scotland missionaries who laid out a few rough holes in some unlikely parts of the bush. These holy men obviously felt a round of golf would not lessen God's opinion of them, but they often got the chance to find out his opinion first hand, sooner than they would have hoped. An example was one Mr Livingstone who built a three-hole course in Rhodesia. During a tribal uprising in 1913 he was killed by the locals who thought this Scots doctor was the original pioneer who had died 40 years before.

The 1938 British team arrive at the South African Ladies' Golf Union Headquarters

SOUTH AFRICA

Life in South Africa was generally more sedate, particularly for the women-folk. A Ladies' National Championship was inaugurated in 1906 and eight years later the South African Ladies' Golf Union was formed.

Diana Fishwick (left) and Diane Pearson (right) find that golf in Africa in 1938 could be rather different to Sunningdale

Two boosts to South African ladies' golf were the immigration of the 1908 British champion, Maud Titterton-Gibb who helped form the Transvaal Ladies' Golf Union, and a tour in 1933 by a team of British golfers. Five years later a South African team was sent to Britain and though they proved highly competent they found themselves to be some way behind the best British players.

After the 1939-45 war, South Africa established a series of test matches with Australia and in 1957 the Australian authorities presented the Opal Trophy to be played for by the two nations.

Despite the imposition of the Gleneagles Agreement which banned South Africa from foreign competition, the South African team were joint second in the 1974 World Tournament and two South African girls Jenny Bruce and Alison Sheard were joint first in the IFG Championship in Columbia.

Individual South African girls have performed creditably overseas, notably Nicky le Roux who won the 1970 Belgian Junior Strokeplay Championship. Alison Sheard became a founder member of the European Women's Tour in 1979, when she won the British Ladies' Open title. Laurette Maritz, US Amateur Player of the Year in 1987, joined the European professional Tour in 1988, when she won her first tournament and was named 'Rookie of the Year'.

KENYA

Kenya, too, is producing many top-class girls, but surprisingly most are coming from the African population who have only taken up the sport in recent years. The country has always been blessed with a perfect climate for golf and established itself as the home of golf on the eastern side of the continent, even back in the days of the coursebuilder-clergymen.

The first courses were Nairobi (1907), Muthaiga (1913) and Railway (1922). These allowed admission to women members who, by tradition, have been restricted to the 'Popsy Bar' in the clubhouse, whilst men-only rooms were commonplace (and still are today).

Originally the Kenya Golf Association controlled ladies' golf and was very helpful to them, but the allocation of handicaps was haphazard. With the increase in immigration of British settlers in the 1930s, LGU methods were accepted and handicapping rationalised by the time the first Kenyan Ladies' Championship was played in 1932. Matters improved further when the Kenya Ladies' Golf Union affiliated to the LGU in 1937.

Fifty years later the Kenya Ladies' Title has become one of the continent's premier events and entries are received from all over Africa, with Mrs Leah Mburu the outstanding modern winner.

GOLFER BEWARE

For all the progress, Africa remains a continent apart from European golf. Until the 1960s, Karen GC near Nairobi had a sign saying 'Beware of lions around some holes' (it was never specified which particular holes were at risk).

Nyanza GC on the shores of Lake Victoria has several interesting local rules: 'If a ball comes to rest in dangerous proximity to a hippopotamus or crocodile, another ball may be dropped at a safe distance no nearer the hole without incurring a penalty stroke.' And 'A ball alighting in a hippo's hoof print merits a free drop.'

The Scots Influence in Europe

The British have often been accused of not being good Europeans, but the Stuart Family were only too glad to embrace Europe when things got rather hot at home in 1688. After which time they proceeded to make a general nuisance of themselves all over the continent. In between political skulduggery, it is recorded in the 1770s that Charles Stuart the Young Pretender was disturbed playing the old game of golf outside his house in Rome.

But by the end of 18th century, the Stuart Family was no longer considered a threat to Britain because of their sheer political ineptitude. Their place as Britain's bogeymen was taken by Napoleon Bonaparte, who indirectly re-started the story of Scotland's influence on European golf.

France

Golf in Napoleonic France began in 1814 amid the pleasant farming country of Pau in the foothills of the Pyrenees. The Duke of Wellington's victorious army came to this district after deposing Napoleon Bonaparte. In the brief lull before Napoleon returned for his Waterloo, a party of red-coated Scots Army officers were stationed in Pau. With little to occupy them, the soldiers soon produced some clubs and balls and indulged in their curious national game. This must have had many a French peasant wondering how such empty-headed individuals could be so effective a fighting force.

The regiment left Pau soon afterwards, but some British ex-patriots remained. These included the Duke of Hamilton and his French-born wife who had a chateau near Pau. The Hamiltons' friends included Colonel and Mrs Hutchinson (of Westward Ho! fame) and after several bottles of rich Bordeaux wine one evening, the idea of a nine-hole course at Pau was mulled over and eventually came into being in 1856.

From the beginning Mrs Hutchinson, the Duchess and other girls were a frequent if incongruous sight over the Pau Course, and even in 1876 when a ladies' link was opened, the ladies preferred the larger fairways. Four years later the main course was increased to 18 holes and the club acquired its first clubhouse. The ladies did not have their own wing until 1898. Appropriately, the first picture to be hung in their wing was the famous portrait of the original women players at Westward Ho!

LES DEMI-PENSIONERS

By the 1900s golf in France had made little progress amongst the indigenous population, but at Biarritz, the first French golfing star had emerged in Arnaud Massy, a Basque. He became the first non-Briton to win the Open Championship. He and his French golfer friends were the exception, for Biarritz GC relied heavily upon well-heeled and well-bred British visitors for its custom.

But only the wealthiest Britons made the long railway journey to the south of France; those who were only 'slightly rich' opted for the courses that were within a day's travel of the Channel ferry ports, such as Dieppe GC, where there were colonies of retired Britons who found that their pensions went further, south of the Channel.

PARIS FASHION

'Les anglais' were less conspicuous in Paris, and here golf established itself as a fashionable new game amongst the well-to-do French men and women. Paris also became the home of the Federation Française de Golf which was created to control both men's and women's golf. In 1908 the FFG organised a Ladies' Close Championship and a year later the Open Ladies' Champion-

Two great French champions from the 1920s – Manette Le Blan and Simone de la Chaume – together at Le Touquet

ship was inaugurated and eventually ranked in prestige just behind the British title.

The French population had all their courses to themselves when the outbreak of the First World War ended British holidays on the Continent. When peace returned the courses remained quiet and youngsters could play and develop without undue hinderance. This freedom produced several outstanding girls, notably Simone de la Chaume, Manette le Blan and Lally Vagliano.

FRENCH VINTAGE

Simone de la Chaume first won acclaim by winning the 1924 British Girls' title at Stoke Poges. She defeated Enid Wilson and Dorothy Pearson. She was a small girl by golfing standards but took the French Close title at fifteen and at seventeen went on to the British Championship as the best player in Europe. Few people gave her a chance against the best American players in 1927 but the Stoke Poges result was exactly repeated with Mlle De le Chaume beating Enid Wilson in the semi-final and Dorothy in the final – the first foreign player to take the British title.

In 1928 Simone unluckily drew Glenna Collett in the first round and lost. This opened the door for her clubmate Manette le Blan to win the title.

French golf had reached dizzy heights and for the first France v Britain Vagliano Cup match, Simone was captain and subsequently represented her country for 22 more seasons.

Her private life was no less successful. At the height of her career she married the great French tennis champion René Lacoste and helped create the Lacoste leisurewear empire. The golden touch proved hereditary with their daughter Catherine becoming a world star in the amateur field, and even triumphing against professionals.

LALLY

FFG President André Vagliano must have begun to doubt the wisdom of his original gift of a trophy for the match between France and Britain, when considering the results of the early years of the competition.

But Monsieur Vagliano made a far greater contribution to his nation's golf through his daughter Vicomtesse Lally de St Sauveur, who was a real aristocrat of the golf course possessing tremendous panache and elegance when hitting a golf ball.

Lally emulated Simone de la Chaume by winning the British Girls title in 1937 and the last French Close championship played before the war. It was nearly a decade before circumstances permitted her to capture the first of her four French Open titles. Later, as Mrs Segard, she established herself as probably the best player in Europe, most noticeably winning the 1950 British Championship at Royal County Down. She was also Swiss, Italian, Spanish and Luxembourg Champion.

The French champion Simone de la Chaume at Stoke Poges

Catherine Lacoste – she said she would be the best and she lived up to her word, winning the 1967 US Women's Open and the 1969 World Amateur title

A French international for nearly 30 years, she appropriately captained Europe in 1959 on the first occasion that the format of the Vagliano Cup was changed to GB v Europe.

BRIGITTE FROM BIARRITZ

Curiously, the British Girls championship has been a remarkable indicator of French golfing talent over the years and in 1957, the title went to Biarritz in the hands of Brigitte Varangot, a small squarely built girl who became the premier European lady golfer of the early 1960s.

She won three British Ladies titles and was considered virtually unbeatable in matchplay and her record at home was comparable with any of her great predecessors.

BRED IN THE PURPLE

The conveyor belt of French talent did not relax with Brigitte Varangot, for Catherine Lacoste emerged with that great French sporting pedigree.

The tall and rangey Miss Lacoste had her mother's capacity to hit the ball an enormous distance and from her father she inherited a tennis champion's stubborn determination to win. As a junior, she lost an important golf match. Catherine was really angry with herself for losing and instead of congratulating her opponent, she went over and said, 'Don't worry, I will prove to be a better player than you ever will.'

With this iron will, she helped France win the inaugural Espirito Santo Trophy in 1964 and was runner-up in the French Close Championship a year later. But even with her superb record in Europe she looked out of her depth in the 1967 US Women's Open at Hot Springs, Virginia, against all the top American professionals. She was determined to make the challenge on her own, refusing to allow her parents to accompany her.

Catherine began steadily and was second on 71 after 18 holes before producing two superb rounds to establish a clear lead. She started the final round knowing steadiness, rather than fireworks, would give her the title. But suddenly, from out of the pack, came Louise Suggs who had been miles adrift but who suddenly managed to conjure up eight birdies in 15 holes. In the face of such a challenge, the young Miss Lacoste kept her nerve and birdied the 17th to be beyond Louise's reach.

Two years later, Catherine established herself as the best amateur of her generation when she won the two French titles and then the Spanish Championship before turning her attention to the British and US Amateur titles.

With the British Championship being held at Royal Portrush, Catherine came over a week early with her mother to practice and progressed through to the final without any alarms. The final was a different matter against the British girl, Ann Irvin.

At the 10th hole Catherine hit a wild drive that was going out of bounds until it struck a spectator and bounced back into play. Ann Irvin lost by only one hole and says philosophically. 'You cannot compete with luck of that magnitude'. Miss Lacoste afterwards thanked the spectator Maureen Skinner for her involuntary help.

A month later, Catherine went over to Los Colinos, Texas, in search of the US Amateur Championship and a unique 'Grand Slam' of amateur golf. She overcame temperatures well above 100 degrees and some formidable opposition before beating Shelley Hamlin in a tense final.

This was Catherine's swan song, having made it clear that she had no intention of turning professional. A year later she married and retired to Spain, becoming the mother of four children.

PREMIER PROFESSIONALS

It would be intriguing to know how Catherine Lacoste would have fared on the WPG European Tour that surfaced soon after her retirement. But in her absence, the professional game has been graced by two top class French girls, Anne-Marie Palli and Marie-Laure de Lorenzi.

Anne-Marie Palli was six times French Amateur Champion and twice

Marie-Laure de Lorenzi – the outstanding European woman player of the late 1980s and a major sporting heroine in France

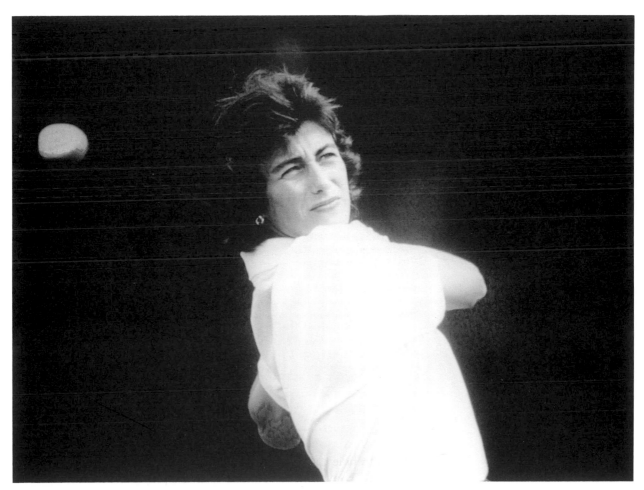

European Junior Champion before joining the US LPGA Tour. Surprisingly, she struggled as a professional, and in her first season won only $600. As a result she lost her tour card. Dropped to the 'Mini-Tour', she reappraised her game, regained her card and promptly recorded a tour win. For the remainder of the 1980s, the Arizona-based girl has been a solid earner on the US LPGA tour.

FRENCH ELEGANCE

One of the major winners in Europe is the tall, elegant and well-groomed Marie-Laure de Lorenzi from Biarritz, whose success is a long way from her childhood when she was adopted by Basque parents. She became one of Europe's top amateurs, and one especially big match was when she married the Spanish Amateur Champion, Roman Taya.

Despite the pressures of marriage and having a little girl, Marie-Laure turned professional and in 1987 immediately won two events. She became the number one player on the European tour for the next two seasons with 11 wins and nearly £180,000 in prize money.

Unfortunately all has not been roses with the failure of her marriage, a victim of her success, and injury problems affecting her game, but she could yet become one of France's finest champions.

FRANCE MAINTENANT

The success of Marie-Laure has led to unprecedented interest and the number of lady golfers in France is doubling every five years. By 1990 there were 55,000 French women players at 635 courses throughout the country and the bulldozers and earthmovers are busy building for the future.

The bulldozers almost destroyed a piece of history in 1988, when it was planned to tear up the old course at Pau and build houses. Fortunately sense prevailed and the old course was saved.

Other European countries with little or no golfing history must look enviously at the old course at Pau.

Switzerland

Switzerland is another country with a golfing history. As ever it began with 19th century British visitors attracted by the high value of sterling against the Swiss franc.

But if the Anglo Saxons sought their summer sun in Biarritz or Pau, it was to the Alps for the winter snow that they all made the two-day rail journey to St Moritz or Davos.

Winter sports such as skating, skiing and tobogganing were as popular amongst the British upper crust, as tennis and golf were in summer. But inevitably the excitement of snow sports and never-ending party-going can pall, and in 1891 the enterprising owner of St Moritz's premier hotel, The

Kulm, built a small nine-hole course to entertain his visitors.

The golfing venture was a great success and over the next decade other hotels opened similar nine-hole courses at Samedan (1898), Montreux-Aigle (1900), Lucerne-Sonnenberg and Axelfels. Interest amongst the visitors was so great that in 1902 they formed the ASG to control golf in Switzerland. Five years later the ASG inaugurated the first men's and women's championships.

The early lists of championship winners shows a preponderance of expatriate names, including three wins in 1907/8/9 for the great Lady Margaret Scott (under her married name of Hamilton-Russell).

During two world wars, Switzerland took neutral status and the absence of British visitors hit Switzerland's golf courses badly. But the visitors returned and the courses reopened. Eventually, however, the fall in the value of sterling succeeded where Hitler and the Kaiser had failed. The visitors no longer had servants or booked for two months at a time. Their absence encouraged the Swiss population to use their own courses and golf flourished with the Swiss Golf Federation being formed. They took over the organisation of ladies' championships.

The rise in golf's prominence since 1945 has seen many new 18-hole courses opened and a new wave of home girl golfers has emerged of international standard, notably Carole Charbonnier, Regine Lautens and Evelyn Orly.

Belgium

Belgium, too, has plenty of golfing history, for its royal patron King Leopold II fell in love with the game whilst visiting Britain. He encouraged the founding of Royal Antwerp GC, in 1888, and nine other 'royal' courses soon afterwards.

A print of golf at Royal Antwerp shows a lady golfer on the 6th tee in 1895, but the ladies made little contact with any trophies until comparatively modern times, when Florence Descampe, Belgium's Match Play champion became European Amateur Champion. Turning professional, she made an immediate impact, by winning the Danish Open in 1988 and finishing second in the 1989 British Open. She won three WPGF events, including the Ladies' Matchplay Title, the following year, and looks to be one of the great stars of the 1990s.

Before Miss Descampe, the only other Belgian girl golfer of note was Liliane de Rethy, who figures more prominently in Italy's golf history.

Italy

Besides the Roman golfing holiday of Bonnie Prince Charlie in the 1770s, no more records of the sport in Italy exist until 1900 when a handful of courses were opened, mainly for foreign visitors.

Golf slowly established itself and in the 1920s, the attractive course at

Villa d'Este near Lake Como became the home of the Italian Ladies' Championship which was dominated by expatriate English girls.

After the Second World War, the Ladies' Championship began to gain stature and was won in 1948 by a genuine princess Liliane de Rethy, who later became the second wife of King Leopold III of the Belgians.

Italy produced its own queen of the golf course soon afterwards in Isa Goldschmid Bevione who was Italian Open champion 10 times and Close champion on 21 occasions between 1946 and 1974. Isa played all over Europe but in more recent times the best known Italian girl golfer is Federica Dassu, sister of professional Baldovino Dassu. Winner of the Italian Championship, she turned professional in 1984, winning two events on the European Tour.

To improve Italy's prospects on the golf course, the Federazione Italiana Golf has developed a feeder system for young girl players starting with the Under 14s (Campionate Pulchine) and progressing to Cadettes, Ragazza and Juniores. An early result has been the emergence of Stefania Croce who was 1986 British Girls' and 1988 Espirito Santo champion.

Other European countries have modest connections with the game's distant past but seem certain to figure in its golden future.

Sweden's Lisalotte Neumann wins the 1988 US Women's Open

Sweden

Sweden is today in the vanguard of the women's professional game through Liselotte Neumann and Helen Alfredsson, but its first course, at Gothenburg GC, opened in 1902.

Soon afterwards, Hovacs GC opened and became the home of the Swedish Ladies' Championship from 1910. Hovacs had its maintenance problems and inclement weather often led to the Championship being cancelled. This discouraged the foreign players from travelling to play in the tournament.

In the early 1930s, the game became more popular in Sweden, many new 18-hole courses were opened and the Ladies' Championship became better organised. This encouraged foreign girls to participate, notably Molly Gourlay who won three Swedish titles.

The Ladies' Championship was revived in 1946 and local girls regained supremacy, principally through Brigit Karlsson and Liv Forsell (Wollin) who was the first Swedish girl to make an impact internationally besides monopolising the home title.

The success of Liv Forsell was a surprise after Swedish golf's low profile and only the emergence of the WPG European Professional Tour brought home the quality of their girls, notably Liselotte Neumann, winner of five events on the European Tour, who joined the LPGA Tour in America and in her first year in 1988 captured the US Women's Open; Helen Alfredsson, winner in her second year on the European Tour of the British Open, and Anna Oxenstierna, winner of the Players Championship in 1989 after three years competing in European tournaments.

STOCKHOLM SICKNESS

Considering the outgoing attitude of the Swedish nation, home seems to figure prominently in the stories of their top girl golfers.

Anna Oxenstierna is a petite, cheerful vicar's wife from Stockholm whose win in the Players Championship she attributed to her host's home cooking.

The major name in Swedish girl's golf has become Liselotte Neumann who after two seasons of great success in Europe decided to take her undoubted talents to America. The first month was agony with terrible homesickness that forced her to take the first plane back to Sweden. After six weeks with her family she resolved to try again and was rewarded with the US Women's Open title.

Since Liselotte's departure for America, Helen Alfredsson has emerged as the top-ranking Swede in Europe but she decided to compete in the US LPGA qualifying school in Texas, only to discover she had forgotten to apply for entry. She could do nothing but pack up and return home.

ST SEVE AND ST BERNARD

Golfing success for Sweden has come through its girls. But new golfing countries like Germany and Spain, have had major wins only from their top men players, which has in some cases created problems for would-be golfing ladies.

Germany

Germany's first golf courses were opened before the turn of the century in Berlin, Wiesbaden and Hamburg, with golf enjoying its greatest popularity in the Hamburg area.

In 1927 the German Ladies' Open was inaugurated but it had a chequered history until the early fifties when it attracted many foreign girls including Jeanne Bisgood, Angela Bonnallack and Bridget Jackson whose domination hardly encouraged local interest.

The National (Close) Championship was consolation to the home girls who lacked the experience to win their Open title. Monika Moller, Monika Gutermann and Marien Petersen were amongst the best winners.

Ironically the best ever German lady golfer could not compete against them, for Gerda Schleed (Boykin) had turned professional and as a consequence competed against men. She finished 4th in their order of merit in 1955 before trying her luck on the US LPGA Tour where she played for a decade and was 3rd in the 1968 US LPGA Championship but sadly failed to win a tour event.

The path to American golfing success was trod with vastly greater success by Bernhard Langer who became Germany's first golfing hero by winning the US Masters. An explosion of interest resulted and a nation with only 90 golf courses suddenly found itself with thousands of men and women golfers with no facilities.

The principal solution for German golf was to begin a massive course building programme and to restrict membership to ladies and gentlemen with existing handicaps. A classic catch-22 situation has arisen because if you cannot play, you cannot get a handicap.

Desperate measures have been used to obtain handicap certificates. Some Germans have arranged holidays in Scotland and immediately on arrival they have joined the local course, their expensive high-fashion sports clothes contrasting with the tweedy old clothes of the locals. But a fortnight later, they have emerged with a highly prized handicap certificate, plus a mountain of new golf equipment purchased from the now smiling professional.

Spain

Alternatively, keen golfing Germans have flown down to the new golf courses of Spain which are quieter than the clubs back home. The only noise there comes from the monotonous rhythm of the ubiquitous sprinkler that fights a daily battle to maintain an island of green amid the gravel and sand.

Spain was a modern convert to the Scots game, and its plethora of new courses were built in the last 20 years to cope with the influx of British holidaymakers arriving at new airports, laden down with golf clubs and duty free liquor.

When the locals, such as Severiano Ballesteros and Jose Maria Olazabal, had the chance to play golf, they proved outstanding, but the supply of Spanish girl golfers has been just a trickle. Only Marta Figueras-Dotti has emerged as world class, winning the 1982 British Women's Open as an amateur.

Daughter of the president of the Spanish Golf Association, she became the first woman professional golfer of Spain, and joined the LPGA Tour in 1984 after graduating from the University of California in 1982. In her best season in 1988 she tied with Nancy Lopez but lost the play-off. As an amateur, she won the Italian, Spanish and French titles, after taking up golf at the age of 8.

SECOND CENTURY

With new courses being built all over Europe and the world, the future for the game is assured but the traditional powerbase of the USA and Britain seem certain to change as they face challenges from new nations. Perhaps the only safe assumption we can make is that the second century of ladies' golf will probably bring as much change as the first.

Part Four

1 The Unfair Sex

During the preparation of this book, it came as a shock to the author and many other people involved in its preparation, how commonly discrimination against women in golf exists and for that matter has always existed. Also, how in the face of such adversity, some clever women have fought back.

This is the story of the prejudice and the pride that has overcome it.

MIDNIGHT CALLER

In the 1980s, an obscure provincial golf writer was asked to write a standard advertising piece about a club's centenary. Eventually the standard 1,000 word article was prepared and sent to the captain for his approval. A few nights later, the writer was aroused from his slumbers when the phone rang. On the other end was a very angry golf club captain.

'You idiot,' he bellowed down the phone.

'What exactly is the matter?' asked the writer.

'This article is wrong.'

'In what respect?'

'You're written that the club has 500 men members, 250 lady members and 25 juniors.'

'Well, they were the figures your secretary provided.'

'Yes, but women are not members. They're FEMALE SUBSCRIBERS. It's bad enough that they are on the premises without allowing them full membership.'

'I'll change the article, but surely it is a minor detail.'

'It may be a minor detail to you, but they'll never get full membership as long as I'm alive.'

To someone who was a member of a golf club created in the 1970s this prejudice against women golfers came as a shock. At many recent clubs, women have equal rights and equal treatment with the men.

OUT OF BOUNDS

At many old and established clubs, women seem to be second-rate citizens who have few rights and who are actively discouraged from taking a full role in the club's activities. This prejudice is justified by explanations that women often pay a slightly reduced subscription. Discrimination comes in many forms. They are excluded from the club's management and many clubrooms are out of bounds to them. In Scotland, until recently, the main lounge of many clubs was closed to women, except on the occasion of the annual mixed foursomes, when they were permitted to accompany their playing partner over the threshold. (Of course, this barrier has never applied to ladies working as barmaids or cleaners.)

On the course many women are unable to play regularly because they work full-time and are therefore unable to play on a Thursday morning, after 10 am, or whenever the club's management committee decrees is suitable – or at least was suitable before the 1914–18 War.

ELSIE'S TALE

Perhaps it is remarkable, in view of the restrictions applied to women's tee times, that the female game ever took off and players such as Cecil Leitch did not just sit at home and do their knitting, instead of inspiring others to emulate their achievements.

An early case of discrimination arose at St Anne's Old Links after they had hosted a memorable English Close Championship in 1919, when the great Cecil won the title. A large crowd of fans followed the champion over the yellow green sandhills, including a tall, well-rounded girl, Elsie Corlett, who had time off from her job at the local tram depot.

In 1921 Elsie Corlett was expelled from St Anne's Old Links for the crime of asking for a handicap certificate. She recovered to become a Curtis Cup regular and an English champion

Elsie was determined to follow in Cecil's footsteps and devoted every spare moment to practising. She used a ball tied to a string in her back garden or hit a battered old object across the windblown sands of Blackpool. Her game improved and she joined Old Links, but her aspirations hit a brick wall when she tried to get an official handicap needed for open competitions. The all-male club committee dismissed the idea as out of the question.

The Ladies' Section considered the matter unfinished, and they wrote a letter to the men asking them to reconsider the request. The Committee were outraged and immediately expelled Elsie and disbanded the Ladies' Section.

There is a happy ending. Miss Corlett crossed the town and joined Royal Lytham and St Annes, and went on to become English Champion and a Curtis Cup regular in the 1930s. Sadly the block on a Ladies' Committee at St Anne's Old Links remained until 1944 when a wartime shortage of manpower (or woman power) necessitated a more liberal approach from the committee.

Recalling her great revolt seventy years later, Elsie puffed on her ever present cigarette and asked that her dark secret be kept quiet whilst she was alive, for fear of upsetting any remaining members of the St Anne's committee (who incidentally would have been over 150 years of age when she died in 1988).

NO DOGS AND WOMEN

Elsie's tale was a true one, but many great legends of the struggle should be treated with a pinch of salt, particularly the sign alleged to hang outside one East of Scotland club which read, 'No Dogs and Women'. This legend certainly dates from the 1930s and may originally have been true, but over the years, the identity of the original club has been lost and whilst everyone has heard the story, no one seems sure of the original home. Certainly the joke has been embroidered by other clubs reproducing the message. Mass-produced copies were available at one time.

Another great legend concerns Leasowe GC on the Wirral, which is alleged to have never allowed a woman in its clubhouse or over its links. The Leasowe secretary says, 'It's a good story but it's a shame the facts spoil a great yarn. The simple truth is that originally we never had a ladies' changing room and they had the embarrassment of changing in the car park. For obvious reasons women could not be bothered and opted to play at other courses with better ladies' facilities.

TRUE STORIES

Genuine cases of discrimination do exist and range from the petty (at Gosforth Park women are forbidden to walk past the main clubhouse window) to the blatantly unfair. An example occurred in 1990, when girls in Durham were excluded from a junior national competition for no other reason than the clubs who hosted the regional heats did not want them on the premises. The clubs defended their bias by saying, 'The girls would want special changing facilities and we couldn't be bothered because there's not many young girl golfers anyway.'

GOING IT ALONE

Possibly there aren't that many girl golfers simply because they are discriminated against and because boys naturally tended to think of girls as 'soppy'. Often, this juvenile bias means young girls must play alone until they reach a reasonable standard.

Perhaps it would reassure these youthful outcasts to know that their problem has been around since 1860, when bands of lady golfers decided anything the men can do, women can definitely do better.

LADIES IN THE CLUB

By tradition in the homeland of golf, women at many of the great Scots golf clubs have been refused any status and were never even allowed over the doorstep until recently. To play golf in Victorian times, numbers of Scottish ladies banded together and formed their own golf clubs. Their task was made easier because the borough councils who owned the local links were prepared to let women play golf alongside the men.

Carnoustie Ladies is the oldest of the survivors dating back to 1868, but the most renowned is St Rule of St Andrews which is not a golf club at all. Strictly speaking, St Rule is a 'club for ladies' which at one time housed the LGU offices and had a large number of golfers amongst its members. These included Agnes Grainger, who formed the Scottish Ladies' Golf Union.

The self-rule trend caught on and a number of these special clubs sprang up in England but despite royal and ancient connections only a handful survived.

MERGERS, HIJACKING AND TAKEOVER BIDS

The ladies of Blackheath were to suffer the fate of their Scots cousins and were barred by England's oldest club, Royal Blackheath. This forced the ladies to form their own club at nearby Barnehurst. However, eventually the two clubs were merged.

The only Royal Ladies' Club, formed at Eastbourne in 1893, suffered an unhappier ending. Forty years later the club was effectively hijacked, when their male neighbours, Royal Eastbourne, formed a ladies' section. An unseemly row developed when the men's club claimed that the ladies had only been given the 'Royal' prefix because King Edward VII had been confused and thought the ladies' club was part of the male organisation.

Another 'Royal' who had a better time with the ladies was Royal Liverpool. The famous Wirral club never admitted ladies inside its ivy clad walls until a ladies' section was formed. Good relations were maintained by members' wives and daughters joining nearby Moreton Ladies which produced two champions in Molly Graham and Lottie Dod. The disappearance under the plough of Moreton in 1915 left a void for local women golfers which was filled by Wirral Ladies.

ON THEIR OWN BEHOOF

Today, Wirral Ladies is one of only three surviving English Ladies' golf clubs (Sunningdale Ladies and Formby Ladies are the others). Wirral Ladies stands on leafy Oxted Common overlooking the wide, grey River Mersey which brought such fabulous wealth to Liverpool in the 19th century.

Pre-eminent in local social circles at the time was Royal Liverpool GC member, George Potter, whose wife provoked a crisis when she decided she would like to play golf. George was in a predicament. Royal Liverpool was one of the finest clubs in the world and not even Potter's wealth could persuade his colleagues to change the rules and admit women.

Today some men may bribe their wives with a new car, but Potter bribed his wife to forget Royal Liverpool, by building a golf course, just for her and her lady friends.

The *Birkenhead Advertiser* on 17th February, 1894, reported, 'The talk is that golfers of the sterner sex are no longer to have their own way at the putting game for Wirral Ladies' GC are now having links prepared on their own behoof. Girl caddies only will be used and male persons are only admitted as

The 1st tee at Sunningdale Ladies' Club

associate members under stringent restrictions.'

A century later the male restrictions are far from stringent and the men seem a happy breed in an organisation commanded by women, and the ladies see nothing unusual in the reversed roles. Outsiders are sometimes confused.

One of Wirral's leading ladies is former Club Captain, Joan Gray, who once went to buy a tractor for the club. The tractor dealer totally ignored her, believing that no woman could be mechanically minded. Eventually she convinced him that she had done her research and knew all about tractors.

As she was leaving with the tractor bought, the dealer kept looking at the cheque and applogising. 'I never imagined I'd meet a woman who actually knew what a tractor was for!'

Twenty years later Joan Grey smiles and admits such male chauvinism was not unusual.

2 Dress

Clothes for women's golf have always been important, but in the early days only the negative aspects were remembered: thou shalt not wear trousers. Thou shalt not dress casually, etc, etc. Gradually matters improved and since the 1950s, manufacturers have recognised ladies' golf as an exciting and lucrative market.

Today, women go to great lengths and expense to avoid dressing the same as their friends, but in the olden days everyone dressed the same. It is therefore something of a miracle the ladies' game developed, when one considers the impracticability of the golfing garb adopted by Issette Pearson or her 1890s companions.

DRESSING DOWN

Although Issette lived on well into the 20th century, she never made any concession to the brave new world. Her domestic staff recall that even at the end she dressed as though Gladstone or Disraeli was still at the helm of the Empire. It took 30 minutes and the attention of several maids to successfuly attach all the corsets, stays, buttons and bows that held together Issette's Victorian outfits. Such clothes may have been socially correct in 1890 but they made no concessions to practicality, least of all to playing golf.

When Issette was one of Britain's top players, ladies' golfing jackets (red in colour at the best clubs) were compulsory. They did at least have pleats in the back to allow for driving from the tee, but had little give, being made of stiff material. The jacket overhung heavily layered skirts of ankle length with the principal matching accessories being nailed leather boots and a straw boater attached to the hair by long pins.

AN AMERICAN IN PARIS

The first hint of change came in 1900 when the Olympic Games were held in Paris. Golf was then amongst the sports on offer. Despite America's then low golfing profile, a Chicago Girl Margaret Abbot comfortably won the Olympic gold medal and always maintained that the only other competitors were French Ladies who encumbered themselves with high heels and tight dresses

which effectively destroyed any chance they had against an opponent who dressed for practicality rather than posturing.

Soon afterwards, another winner – 'Miss Higgins' – also emerged from across the Atlantic. Miss Higgins was no lady, it was a useful elastic attachment to stop the voluminous skirts of lady golfers flapping in the wind. By attaching round the legs, it made seeing the ball remotely possible and hitting the ball far easier; walking was virtually impossible however. It took its name from its inventor, one of the top US lady players.

In Britain, a clever lady from Yelverton GC in Devon invented a leather skirt hem that afforded some protection from brambles and hedges. Such inventions were important as ladies' golf moved from the putting green on to the open links.

It is something of a miracle that the ladies' game developed, considering the impracticality of golfing garb in 1900

STEMMING THE TWEEDY FLOW

The new breed of golfing girls replacing Issette found great use for adjustable hem straps and buttons, but the old style of Norfolk jackets lingered on and would have survived much longer, but for the Great War that propelled womanhood from drawing room to drawing pay.

An entire generation of young men died on the battlefields of Europe and left society with a huge void. Who would perform the tasks that the dead manhood would have normally done? There was only one answer.

Women pushed pens, drove buses and dug the land. They were promoted into spheres of activity they had not dreamed of entering before and they tried to compromise their new status with good dress sense. Practicality with style was the order of the day. They adopted clothes that allowed them to get on with the job. Tweed suits with long skirts, shirts and ties became almost a uniform for the new breed of women.

During the Roaring Twenties, women rejected the old drab styles in favour of shorter skirts and the 'bandeau'

TWENTIES VISION

The changes wrought by the Great War did not just go away – too much had changed. Not least, the Americans had come to Europe for war and stayed for the peace. They opened factories that preached the mass-production of clothes.

Working women had money to spend on clothes and they played their part as the Roaring Twenties rejected the darkness and depression of war in a blaze of colour and excitement. The fashions they chose were shorter skirts without bosom and waistline, and (heaven forbid) the legs were visible. This fashion crept on to the golf course where the casual look was promoted by Cecil Leitch, who was the first woman to dress comfortably for golf and who also adopted the hair band or 'bandeau' favoured by the tennis stars.

The golfing authorities fought against this tide of 'decadence' by banning extravagant clothes, especially golf skirts with decorative pleats and they forbade ladies not wearing stockings, or rolling up their sleeves during the summer months!

LEADERS ON THE BOARDS

Despite these ultimatums and the excitement of the Roaring Twenties, the golf authorities did not have to face anarchy on the links. As 'Vogue', the trendy US fashion magazine recorded, 'In Britain, most lady golfers continue to appear in crumpled pullovers, shapeless skirts and deplorable hats and shoes.' And one fashion commentator remarked that British Ladies' golf clothes came in just three shades: dull, dark and drab.

Across the Atlantic things were changing. Lady golfers could buy golfing slacks, 'plus fours' and trouser-skirts and an august US golfing organisation expressed concern that, 'Lady golfers are looting the wardrobes of their husbands and brothers.'

Perhaps the only item of apparel that came out of the male closet and stayed visible was the sweater which was successfully absorbed into ladies' golf and ultimately became a part of high fashion.

A RETURN TO FEMININITY

The worry that women were starting to wear the golfing trousers and were losing their femininity was soon over, as the 1930s fashions saw greater emphasis on the female figure.

Many of the new fashions from Paris and New York were impractical for the golf course, notably the small brimmed hat promoted by the great movie stars. It was great for Belair, but hopeless for Belhaven, being easily dislodged by a gust of wind. Not surprisingly, it gave way to the inexpensive but functional beret, which was so closely associated with Scotland's champion Helen Holm.

The black beret exemplified the notion that dark conservative clothes should be worn for golf, and this remained unchallenged, with tweed still first choice for skirts and jackets, especially in winter. In summer a sense of gay abandon developed, with sleeveless tops and dark woollen skirts being popular. Golfing slacks remained an unacceptable 'Americanism', but they did produce one of the most colourful characters in golfing history: Gloria Minoprio.

ST GLORIA

The tall dark Miss Minoprio's claim to fame was that she was the first woman to wear slacks on a British golf course.

Miss Minoprio, a former conjuror's assistant, had joined Littlestone GC in 1931 but had never entered a competition organised by the Kent club. She always entered the slightly more competitive English Close Championship. She had more success in entering golfing legend in October, 1933. A joker suggested something important must have happened that bright Monday morning because the golfing press were up and about by 10 am – a virtually unheard of event. Sure enough, Gloria arrived in a yellow Rolls Royce wearing a beret, turtle neck sweater and matching black trousers. She never said a word, and handed two clubs to her caddy; she never played with more than one club in a round and the caddy's job was to carry the spare. Not surprisingly she failed to qualify.

The LGU coped with this eccentric behaviour by issuing a declaration that 'deplored any departure from the traditional costume of ladies', and Henry Longhurst was heard to comment 'Sic Transit Gloria Monday'.

(Gloria continued to be a thorn in the LGU's side, until the outbreak of war when she married a Polish gentleman and moved to Vancouver where she died in the late 1950s.)

Dorothy Minoprio – the first British woman to wear trousers for a major competition

VIRTUE OF NECESSITY

Ironically, as Gloria Minoprio departed for Canada, shortages meant women could wear slacks and other functional clothes for the first time in public. The authorities had to promote the idea that sensible clothes were the only way to overcome wartime shortages, and that they could be smart and stylish. The message was to make a virtue out of necessity.

When peace came, Britain's once flourishing sportswear and fashion industries had been flattened as badly as any bombed town. It took a decade of peace for them to recover with the government's order that luxury goods were now a low priority.

Industry and fashion in America recovered far quicker, and English

In 1975 the mini skirt appeared, briefly, during the Colgate European Open at Sunningdale. On the left is a young Jan Stephenson

Champion Jeanne Bisgood recalls the shock of her Curtis Cup colleagues when they went to Buffalo, NY, in 1950 and saw nylon stockings on sale without rationing coupons. And at Royal Porthcawl in Wales, there was a record number of entries for the ladies' medal when it was announced that the first prize was a pair of nylon stockings!

Life at home was grim; petrol was rationed forcing ladies to cycle everywhere which again meant opting for suitable clothes, but at least the new wonder material, 'nylon', guaranteed your clothes would not crease (even if they were covered with grease from your bicycle chain).

THROW AWAY YOUR OLD IRONS

By the end of the 1950s, the only grease about was on men's hair, as the fashion industry discovered youth and began aiming its products towards their end of the market. In particular towards the young females with money to spend on bright new clothes. Gradually the bright colours that were reserved for discotheques and coffee bars began to appear on the golf course. Nothing was sacred, even the humble golfing sock began to take on gaudy shades though fortunately this coincided with the marketing of a fresh air spray for golfers with over-ripe socks. Everything was changing (except for some people's socks), and the golf course became the home for such short-lived (and often short-length) fads as the mini-skirt, hot-pants, anoraks and ponchos. But in many clubs, one fashion has been consistently banned – jeans, either on course or in the clubhouse.

FULL CIRCLE

By the 1980s the marketing and advertising of ladies' (and men's) golf equipment had become a huge industry. Golf shops were bound to copy the bright and breezy styles of the high street shops. They ceased to be dark and dingy places, with the central feature being a 19th-century lathe surrounded by a collection of every old golf club every produced. They now had racks of lovely clothes and new fabrics.

Market leader in the professional shop became the humble woollen sweater which had first found favour in the 1930s and was now back in checks, diamonds and every conceivable colour and pattern.

3 Equipment and Facilities

T̲he successful growth of the game of golf is not entirely due to great players or organisers. The main reason for its success has been the development of the ball, the clubs and the other inanimate objects that put the game in the reach (and the pocket) of anyone with reasonable co-ordination.

Golf was not always so accessible as it is today. In former times, equipment was crude and expensive. Matters improved because individuals tried innovations, even though they often met with hostility for their efforts.

Our final chapter therefore celebrates the pioneers and indeed all the sport's ephemera whose development has affected ladies' golf. Where else can we begin, but with the one event that started the modern game – the introduction of the first proper golf ball.

FIRST, ADDRESS THE BALL

Golf as a game was virtually impossible whilst the feathery and wooden golf balls were the limits of technology. In the 1840s the fore-runner of the present ball, the 'gutty', was introduced by John W Patterson. He was an Edinburgh wood and ivory turner, whose missionary brother James had brought back from India some pliable gummy material called 'gutta percha'. The new golf ball made from the gum was nicknamed the 'gutty'. It revolutionised golf because it was cheap, durable and easy to make.

But it hit the original professional golfers in the pocket, the most painful spot to a true Scot. Previously golf balls had been made by a tiny number of individuals who charged 10/- (50p) for a feathery; now the Patterson brothers sold the far more durable gutty for one shilling (5p). Despite the hostility, the new ball was soon on sale in London and another brother, Robert, took some 'gutties' to America in 1850.

The 'gutty' was far from perfect, not least, because in winter it became like a lump of concrete and had to be softened up in warm water before play. Many people tried to improve the 'gutty', before a golfing dentist Coburn Haskell, of Cleveland, Ohio, had a brainwave whilst playing with a baseball, which was made of wool tightly wound round a solid core. Haskell realised that a variation of the baseball could be introduced to golf by winding together rubber strands. The 'Haskell ball' was not as hard to hit and went further than the 'gutty'; but it was easily damaged and took three weeks of glueing, painting and marking before it was ready for the shops.

TECHNOLOGY

Throughout the 20th century manufacturers tried to improve on Haskell's basic concept but little progress was made until 1965. The Dunlop 65 – named to mark Henry Cotton's record round when winning the 1934 Open at Royal St George's – became the most popular and profitable golf ball for decades.

Competition to produce the best selling golf ball has been fierce and expensive, with millions of dollars being spent on developing a new ball such as the new DDH (dodecahedron) ball whch goes 20 yards further than the balls produced in the 1970s (but only if you play like Laura Davies).

Various attempts have been made to market a golf ball purely for women's golf, notably the Lady Player and the Flying Lady brands that appeared in the 1970s. Such attempts have met with little success and the ladies have been happy to adopt the regulation 1.68 ball used throughout the game.

COLLECTA-BALLS

A surprisingly buoyant market in old golf balls has developed in recent years with $10,000 changing hands for a pre-Patterson 'feathery'. Even modern balls with corroborating proof of connections to some golfing great can bring thousands of pounds at auction.

In th 1970s Severiano Ballesteros presented a golf ball he had used to win the Open title to an English friend and inscribed the ball with a goodwill message and the date.

The valuable ball sat on the friend's desk at home for some months until he went abroad for a week. He returned to find the ball gone. Frantically, he ran upstairs to his wife and asked if she had seen it.

'Of course, I used it for a ladies fourball last Thursday and lost it in the pond. It looked so scruffy, I knew you would not want to use it yourself!'

BUGGIES

If women played a secondary role in the invention of the ball, at least a woman is credited with inventing the first golf buggy. This clever lady was a New York dog trainer who, in 1903, taught dogs to pull buggy cars across golf courses. Not surprisingly this dog-sledge idea failed to catch on because there are too many trees on the average golf course and dogs will be dogs.

It was left to a man, Lyman Beecher of Florida, to perfect the golf buggy but he too had his problems. His prototype buggy had six batteries, weighed a quarter of a ton and invariably ran out of juice miles from the clubhouse. His persistence paid off, however, and today the buggy has become an essential part of American golf course life, even if in Britain most players prefer to walk – or hire that most inanimate of objects: a caddy.

CADDIES

Caddies are a breed apart, who have enriched the history of golf and whole books have been written about them, or, more accurately, their foibles.

In the early days, the sport was prohibited on Sundays not because of its spiritual damage to golfers but because it entailed the caddy having to work on the Lord's Day. Getting them to work the rest of the week could be difficult. In 1900, two caddies were prosecuted for refusing to work for lady visitors and another caddy was sacked for breaking into fits of laughter everytime one lady golfer tried to hit the ball.

Lady and men golfers could suffer badly at the hands of these hired hands, for many caddies failed to grasp the basic concept of the employer/employee relationship. This, despite the training they underwent from the caddymaster, and more importantly, being paid as 1st or 2nd class caddies.

Their behaviour was, in theory, tightly controlled but they could be an irascible bunch, who often spent a good portion of their income on strong drink, which presumably made the bad times bearable. There could however be good times, as witnessed by an ancient rule at Woodenbridge GC, Co Wicklow, that any player who had a hole-in-one had to pay the caddy 10/- (50p), a huge sum when 4d (1½p) was the going rate for 18 holes.

Unfortunately being a caddy was hardly a career, and the Ministry of Labour in 1913 tried to direct caddies to more regular work and proposed to

The main reason for the successful growth of golf has been the development of the equipment. Since the early 19th century clubs and balls in particular have gradually changed and improved

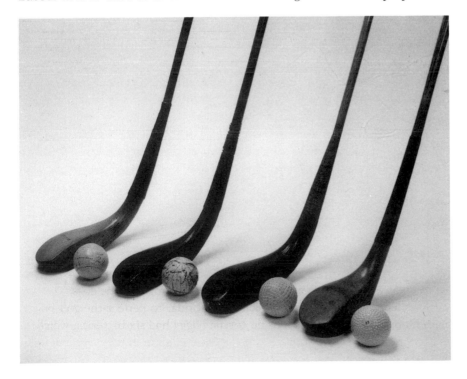

151

ban from caddying anyone who refused a regular job.

Other towns were not so discerning. At St Andrews, the local magistrate once condemned the new fangled education laws that were 'over-educating caddies'. At Silloth the schools closed on Thursdays so that local boys and girls could act as caddies for visitors arriving on the 'Golfers Special' train from Carlisle. Other clubs and towns were neutral such as Wilpshire GC near Blackburn, which issued an instruction telling caddies not to walk on the putting greens wearing clogs.

Clogs and caddies have almost disappeared in the wake of full employment, but caddies still exist at the highest level. Top professional Laura Davies started by caddying for her brother, but the roles were soon reversed when she proved to be the better player.

Other top women professionals are not so fortunate, and must recruit friends to pull their trolleys. Anna Oxenstierna won the WPG European Players Tournament with her landlady as caddy. The landlady asked Anna what this entailed?

'Complete silence from first tee to final green,' replied the player.

THE CLUBHOUSE

Caddies tended to be familiar figures hovering outside clubhouses, perpetual outsiders, as variable as the clubhouses themselves which can range from castles to old shacks.

St Anne's Old Links which hosted the first Ladies' Championship had a wheel-less old tram car as its original home. But St Anne's was unusual, for many old golf clubs tended to use a nearby pub as their gathering place, often buying it when funds permitted. Such buildings were primitive, with the men's facilities consisting of a bar (of course), a tub and primitive toilet facilities. The ladies were usually relegated to a shack out back.

Old time golfers of both sexes were hardy souls. At some seaside courses men and women players would have a dip in the sea if no bathing facilities were available.

At the other end of the Victorian golfing spectrum, the top clubs such as Minchinhampton had the best of everything – even for the ladies. They stipulated in 1899 to the clubhouse builder, that the ladies' facilities were to have priority due to the impending visit of the Midland Ladies' Championship.

THE STORY OF THE THREE LITTLE PIGS

The employment of builders was rare. Most men's clubhouses were built of wood and with so many cigarette, pipe and tobacco smokers about, the premises were invariably destroyed by fire. Women, being tidier and more responsible than the male of the species, often picked a brick building on better sites for their premises. Gullane Ladies' clubhouse was so superior to the men's premises, that the men eventually moved in with the ladies.

Gullane attracts thousands of visitors every year and has always been a prosperous golfing area. Many rural clubs are less fortunate however, and have to keep the club going on a limited income.

A communal bar and one changing room each for men and women is standard accommodation. Funds are boosted by using an honesty box for visitors' green fees. None went to the extent of Easingwold in Yorkshire, which in the 1960s, left the bar unlocked and asked visitors to put their drinks money in the till. Easingwold reported they always seemed to make a profit, because players never had the right change and left more than they owed.

Another clubhouse user, who left more than she should, was a Scots lady who was reprimanded in the 1950s by her club committee for allowing her motor bike to drip oil on the clubhouse floor and disfigure the linoleum. The lesson being that in even the most modest clubhouse, ladies should think twice before taking their motorbikes inside the main lounge.

BETTING ALLOWED IN CLUBHOUSE

Amongst the clubs who came into the modest clubhouse category are several great names of the past. Musselburgh may have held the first ladies' golf competition in 1810, but today the famous old links share their sport with a racecourse and Musselburgh Links golfers operate from the old Tote betting office. (Musselburgh Links should not be confused with the stately grandeur of nearby Royal Musselburgh.)

LAST BUT NOT LEAST, THE GOLF CLUB

If modern day Musselburgh Links are a disappointment, so are many of the golden legends of ancient golf. Not least, the portrait of the old time professional in his shop in Bonnie Scotland, whittling away to produce a classic wooden club from a branch he had just cut from a nearby tree.

This is an attractive idea, but there are hardly any trees around many of the old Scottish courses and most of the woodwork would not make a decent fire never mind a decent golf club. 200 years ago, tiny numbers of golf professionals in Scotland may have made woods from one piece of material, but they used mainly imported woods: beech or malacca for the head and Tennessee hickory for the shaft.

By 1890, the golfing press was already full of letters bemoaning the decline in the clubmaker's art amongst professionals. The letters attacked the small factories that made heads and shafts for professionals to piece together. This minor technological change was repugnant even then to the purist, but it was tiny in scale compared to modern production.

It was on the small scale because the number of golfers was tiny and, to an old timer, a full set of clubs meant something totally different to the modern equivalent. The old set was Driver, Brassie, Spoon, Baffy, Mashie, Jigger, Mashie Niblick and Niblick which roughly equated to Wood through to short iron. Full sets of these were produced but most men and women golfers used a pencil bag containing half a dozen odd clubs.

Some women used altered men's clubs, but from the 1920s 'ladies' sets' were available. These had the same angle of clubface, but with shafts that were shorter and lighter, which caused more whip than men's clubs. You needed Cecil Leitch's talent to cope with their whippiness, but she coped well enough and became champion using only five clubs in her bag. Cecil encouraged lesser players to copy her example by starting county competitions for players using only five clubs. The competitions are still a feature of English golf today.

In Cecil's heyday the role of the club professional was more significant because repairs were more common and hardly anyone else sold golf equiment. Joyce Wethered remembers that the clubs with which she won her championships were acquired from various professionals' shops by trial and error. She would see a club she liked, try it and possibly buy it. Ironically Joyce later gave her name to an early set of ladies' clubs which helped set the trend to mass-marketing.

One mass-marketed American invention Joyce disliked was the metal shafted club which appeared in the 1930s. She commented that it made the game too easy for poor players. But the metal shaft became popular because it was cheap and hard wearing, and when the big American club manufactures started offering huge money rewards in the form of sponsorship to any tournament professional who used their metal-shafted club to win a PGA event, the metal was cast.

CLUBBY CHECKER

Today, club manufacturing and sales are an industry worth hundreds of millions of pounds. The top men and women players are paid huge sums by manufacturers to use and promote only one type of club. This often causes a loss of form by the player who after years of using the same old clubs, dislikes the feel of new clubs. Quietly he or she starts slipping old clubs into the bag and ends up with an assortment of old and trusted favourites. To counteract the re-emergence of this practice, the services of 'club-checkers' are used at US LPGA tournaments to make random checks on the clubs in a players' bag.

Another throwback to times gone by has been the re-emergence of women as clubmakers and repairers. In Victorian times, working wives and daughters were an integral feature of the professional's shop. Today, women such as Margaret Buchman of Delray, Florida, have emerged amongst the best club repairers in America with a list of customers that includes Severiano Ballesteros and Raymond Floyd.

Perhaps if the golden age of clubmaking ever existed, it would be the wife whittling away in the shop while the professional was in the nineteenth, regaling his cronies with comments like, 'Women, what have they ever done for golf?'

Appendices

Ladies' British Open Amateur Championship

Year	Winner	Runner-up	Venue	By
1893	Lady Margaret Scott	Miss Isette Pearson	St Annes	7 and 5
1894	Lady Margaret Scott	Miss Isette Pearson	Littlestone	3 and 2
1895	Lady Margaret Scott	Miss E Lythgoe	Portrush	5 and 4
1896	Miss Pascoe	Misss L Thomson	Hoylake	3 and 2
1897	Miss EC Orr	Miss Orr	Gullane	4 and 2
1898	Miss L Thomson	Miss EC Neville	Yarmouth	7 and 5
1899	Miss M Hezlet	Miss Magill	Newcastle Co Down	2 and 1
1900	Miss Adair	Miss Neville	Westward Ho!	6 and 5
1901	Miss Graham	Miss Adair	Aberdovey	3 and 1
1902	Miss M Hezlet	Miss E Neville	Deal	19th hole
1903	Miss Adair	Miss F Walker-Leigh	Portrush	4 and 3
1904	Miss L Dod	Miss M Hezlet	Troon	1 hole
1905	Miss B Thompson	Miss ME Stuart	Cromer	3 and 2
1906	Mrs Kennon	Miss B Thompson	Burnham	4 and 3
1907	Miss M Hezlet	Miss F Hezlet	Newcastle Co Down	2 and 1
1908	Miss M Titterton	Miss D Campbell	St Andrews	19th hole
1909	Miss D Campbell	Miss F Hezlet	Birkdale	4 and 3
1910	Miss Grant Suttie	Miss L Moore	Westward Ho!	6 and 4
1911	Miss D Campbell	Miss V Hezlet	Portrush	3 and 2
1912	Miss G Ravenscroft	Miss S Temple	Turnberry	3 and 2

(Final played over 36 holes after 1912)

Year	Winner	Runner-up	Venue	By
1913	Miss M Dodd	Miss Chubb	St Annes	8 and 6
1914	Miss C Leitch	Miss G Ravenscroft	Hunstanton	2 and 1

1915-18 No Championship owing to Great War
1919 Should have been played at Burnham in October, but abandoned owing to Railway Strike

Year	Winner	Runner-up	Venue	By
1920	Miss C Leitch	Miss Molly Griffiths	Newcastle Co Down	7 and 6
1921	Miss C Leitch	Miss J Wethered	Turnberry	4 and 3
1922	Miss J Wethered	Miss C Leitch	Prince's, Sandwich	9 and 7
1923	Miss D Chambers	Miss A Macbeth	Burnham, Somerset	2 holes
1924	Miss J Wethered	Mrs Cautley	Portrush	7 and 6
1925	Miss J Wethered	Miss C Leitch	Troon	37th hole
1926	Miss C Leitch	Mrs Garon	Harlech	8 and 7
1927	Miss Thion de la Chaume (France)	Miss Pearson	Newcastle Co Down	5 and 4
1928	Miss Manette Le Blan (France)	Miss S Marshall	Hunstanton	3 and 2
1929	Miss J Wethered	Miss G Collett (USA)	St Andrews	3 and 1
1930	Miss D Fishwick	Miss G Collett (USA)	Formby	4 and 3
1931	Miss E Wilson	Miss W Morgan	Portmarnock	7 and 6
1932	Miss E Wilson	Miss CPR Montgomery	Saunton	7 and 6
1933	Miss E Wilson	Miss D Plumpton	Gleneagles	5 and 4
1934	Mrs AM Holm	Miss P Barton	Porthcawl	6 and 5
1935	Miss W Morgan	Miss P Barton	Newcastle Co Down	3 and 2
1936	Miss P Barton	Miss B Newell	Southport and Ainsdale	5 and 6

1937	Miss J Anderson	Miss D Park	Turnberry	6 and 4
1938	Mrs AM Holm	Miss E Corlett	Burnham	4 and 3
1939	Miss P Barton	Mrs T Marks	Portrush	2 and 1
1940-45 *No Championship owing to Second World War*				
1946	Mrs GW Hetherington	Miss P Garvey	Hunstanton	1 hole
1947	Mrs George Zaharias (USA)	Miss J Gordon	Gullane	5 and 4
1948	Miss Louise Suggs (USA)	Miss J Donald	Lytham St Annes	1 hole
1949	Miss Frances Stephens	Mrs Val Reddan	Harlech	5 and 4
1950	Vicomtesse de Saint Sauveur (France)	Mrs G Valentine	Newcastle Co Down	3 and 2
1951	Mrs PG MacCann	Miss Frances Stephens	Broadstone	4 and 3
1952	Miss Moira Paterson	Miss Frances Stephens	Troon	39th hole
1953	Miss Marlene Stewart (Canada)	Miss P Garvey	Porthcawl	7 and 6
1954	Miss Frances Stephens	Miss E Price	Ganton	4 and 3
1955	Mrs G Valentine	Miss B Romack (USA)	Portrush	7 and 6
1956	Miss Margaret Smith (USA)	Miss Mary P Janssen (USA)	Sunningdale	8 and 7
1957	Miss P Garvey	Mrs G Valentine	Gleneagles	4 and 3
1958	Mrs G Valentine	Miss E Price	Hunstanton	1 hole
1959	Miss E Price	Miss B McCorkindale	Ascot	37th hole
1960	Miss B McIntyre (USA)	Miss P Garvey	Harlech	4 and 2
1961	Mrs AD Spearman	Miss DJ Robb	Carnoustie	7 and 6
1962	Mrs AD Spearman	Mrs MF Bonallack	Birkdale	1 hole
1963	Miss B Varangot (France)	Miss P Garvey	Newcastle Co Down	3 and 1
1964	Miss C Sorenson (USA)	Miss BAB Jackson	Prince's, Sandwich	37th hole
1965	Miss V Varangot (France)	Mrs I Robertson	St Andrews	4 and 3
1966	Miss E Chadwick	Miss V Saunders	Ganton	3 and 2
1967	Miss E Chadwick	Miss M Everard	Harlech	1 hole
1968	Miss B Varangot (France)	Mrs C Rubin (France)	Walton Heath	20th hole
1969	Miss C Lacoste (France)	Miss A Irvin	Portrush	1 hole
1970	Miss D Oxley	Mrs IC Robertson	Gullane	1 hole
1971	Miss Michelle Walker	Miss B Huke	Alwoodley	3 and 1
1972	Miss Michelle Walker	Mrs C Rubin (France)	Hunstanton	2 holes
1973	Miss A Irvin	Miss Michelle Walker	Carnoustie	3 and 2
1974	Miss C Semple (USA)	Mrs A Bonallack	Porthcawl	2 and 1
1975	Mrs N Syms (USA)	Miss S Cadden	St Andrews	3 and 2
1976	Miss C Panton	Miss A Sheard	Silloth	1 hole
1977	Mrs A Uzielli	Miss V Marvin	Hillside	6 and 5
1978	Miss E Kennedy (Australia)	Miss J Greenhalgh	Notts	1 hole
1979	Miss M Madill	Miss J Lock (Australia)	Nairn	2 and 1
1980	Mrs A Sander (USA)	Mrs L Wollin (Sweden)	Woodhall Spa	3 and 1
1981	Mrs IC Robertson	Miss W Aitken	Conwy	20th hole
1982	Miss K Douglas	Miss G Stewart	Walton Heath	4 and 2
1983	Mrs J Thornhill	Miss R Lautens (Switzerland)	Silloth	4 and 2
1984	Miss J Rosenthal (USA)	J Brown	Royal Troon	4 and 3
1985	Miss L Behan (Eire)	C Waite	Ganton	1 hole
1986	Miss McGuire (NZ)	L Briars (Australia)	West Sussex	2 and 1
1987	Miss J Collingham	Miss S Shapcott	Harlech	19th hole
1988	Miss J Furby	J Wade	Deal	4 and 3
1989	Miss H Dobson	E Farquhoson	Royal Liverpool	6 and 5
1990	Mrs J Hall	H Wadsworth	Dunbar	3 and 2

USGA Women's Amateur

Year	Winner	Year	Winner
1895	Mrs Charles S Brown	1907	Margaret Curtis
1896	Beatrix Hoyt	1908	Katherine C Harley
1897	Beatrix Hoyt	1909	Dorothy I Campbell
1898	Beatrix Hoyt	1910	Dorothy I Campbell
1899	Ruth Underhill	1911	Margaret Curtis
1900	Frances C Griscom	1912	Margaret Curtis
1901	Genevieve Hecker	1913	Gladys Ravenscroft
1902	Genevieve Hecker	1914	Katherine Jackson
1903	Bessie Anthony	1915	Florence Vanderbeck
1904	Georgianna M Bishop	1916	Alexa Stirling
1905	Pauline Mackay	1917-18 — *No championships*	
1906	Harriot S Curtis	1919	Alexa Stirling

Year	Winner	Year	Winner
1920	Alexa Stirling	1957	JoAnne Gunderson
1921	Marion Hollins	1958	Anne Quast
1922	Glenna Collett	1959	Barbara McIntire
1923	Edith Cummings	1960	JoAnne Gunderson
1924	Dorothy Campbell Hurd	1961	Anne Quast Decker
1925	Glenna Collett	1962	JoAnne Gunderson
1926	Helen Stetson	1963	Anne Quast Welts
1927	Miriam Burns Horn	1964	Barbara McIntire
1928	Glenna Collett	1965	Jean Ashley
1929	Glenna Collett	1966	JoAnne Carner
1930	Glenna Collett	1967	Mary Lou Dill
1931	Helen Hicks	1968	JoAnne Carner
1932	Virginia Van Wie	1969	Catherine Lacoste
1933	Virginia Van Wie	1970	Martha Wilkinson
1934	Virginia Van Wie	1971	Laura Baugh
1935	Glenna Collett Vare	1972	Mary Budke
1936	Pamela Barton	1973	Carol Semple
1937	Estelle Lawson Page	1974	Cynthia Hill
1938	Patty Berg	1975	Beth Daniel
1939	Betty Jameson	1976	Donna Horton
1940	Betty Jameson	1977	Beth Daniel
1941	Elizabeth Hicks Newell	1978	Cathy Sherk
1942-45 — No championships		1979	Carolyn Hill
1946	Babe Zaharias	1980	Juli Inkster
1947	Louise Suggs	1981	Juli Inkster
1948	Grace S Lenczyk	1982	Juli Inkster
1949	Dorothy Porter	1983	Joanne Pacillo
1950	Beverly Hanson	1984	Deb Richard
1951	Dorothy Kirby	1985	Michiko Hattori
1952	Jacqueline Pung	1986	Kay Cockerill
1953	Mary Lena Faulk	1987	Kay Cockerill
1954	Barbara Romack	1988	Pearl Sinn
1955	Patricia A Lesser	1989	Vicki Goetze
1956	Marlene Stewart	1990	P Hirst

USGA Women's Open

Year	Winner	Year	Winner
1946	Patty Berg	1969	Donna Caponi
1947	Betty Jameson	1970	Donna Caponi
1948	Babe Zaharias	1971	JoAnne Carner
1949	Louise Suggs	1972	Susie Maxwell Berning
1950	Babe Zaharias	1973	Susie Maxwell Berning
1951	Betsy Rawls	1974	Sandra Haynie
1952	Louise Suggs	1975	Sandra Palmer
1953	Betsy Rawls	1976	JoAnne Carner
1954	Babe Zaharias	1977	Hollis Stacy
1955	Fay Crocker	1978	Hollis Stacy
1956	Kathy Cornelius	1979	Jerilyn Britz
1957	Betsy Rawls	1980	Amy Alcott
1958	Mickey Wright	1981	Pat Bradley
1959	Mickey Wright	1982	Janet Alex
1960	Betsy Rawls	1983	Jan Stephenson
1961	Mickey Wright	1984	Hollis Stacy
1962	Murle Lindstrom	1985	Kathy Baker
1963	Mary Mills	1986	Jane Geddes**
1964	Mickey Wright	1987	Laura Davies**
1965	Carol Mann	1988	Liselotte Neumann
1966	Sandra Spuzich	1989	Betsy King
1967	Catherine Lacoste*	1990	Betsy King
1968	Susie Maxwell Berning		

*Amateur   **Won playoff

Wonderful Worplesdon

In the first half of the 20th Century, the calendar of top level ladies' golf was limited to half a dozen major competitions which began with the Avia Foursomes in March (where hot soup was provided at halfway to revive frozen fingers) and ended with the Worplesdon Foursomes in October.

It was in 1921 that an ambitious Colonel Ambrose proposed to the club council that it hold an end of season Men's Open, Ladies' Open and Mixed Foursomes. The Men's and Women's Opens never captured the attention in the way that the Foursomes grabbed the imagination of thousands of spectators who flocked to the tiny village outside Woking to see the greatest names in European golf.

Perhaps the secret of its success lay in the great champion who became inextricably linked with Worplesdon. Joyce Wethered won the first of her nine titles in 1922 partnered by her brother Roger. Joyce was a national heroine and her attendance guaranteed headlines, especially when other great golfing names such as Cecil Leitch, Bernard Darwin, Cyril Tolley and Michael Scott also played.

Worplesdon Foursomes Winners

Year	Winner	Year	Winner
1921	Miss EE Helme & TA Torrance	1959	Miss J Robertson & Innes Wright
1922	Miss J Wethered & RH Wethered	1960	Miss BAB Jackson & MJ Burgess
1923	Miss J Wethered & CJH Tolley	1961	Mrs R Smith & B Critchley
1924	Miss DR Fowler & E Noel Layton	1962	Vicomtesse de St Sauveur & DW Frame
1925	Miss C Leitch & E Esmond	1963	Mrs G Valentine & JE Behrend
1926	Mlle S De La Chaume & RH Wethered	1964	Mrs G Valentine & JE Behrend
1927	Miss J Wethered & CJH Tolley	1965	Mrs G Valentine & JE Behrend
1928	Miss J Wethered & JSF Morrison	1966	Mrs CA Barclay & DJ Miller
1929	Miss M Gourlay & Major CO Hezlet	1967	Mlle C Lacoste & JF Gancedo
1930	Miss M Gourlay & Major CO Hezlet	1968	Miss D Oxley & J Dudok van Heel
1931	Miss J Wethered & Hon. M Scott	1969	Mrs R Ferguson & WS Wilson
1932	Miss J Wethered & RH Oppenheimer	1970	Miss S Roberts & RL Glading
1933	Miss J Wethered & B Darwin	1971	Mrs D Frearson & A Smith
1934	Miss M Gourlay & TA Torrance	1972	Miss B leGarreres & CA Strong
1935	Miss G Craddock-Hartopp & JE Craddock-Hartopp	1973	Miss T Perkins & RJ Evans
		1974	Miss S Birley & RL Glading
1936	Miss J Wethered & Hon. TWE Coke	1975	Mr & Mrs J Thornhill
1937	Mrs HM Heppel & LG Crawley	1976	Mrs B Lewis & JJN Caplan
1938	Mrs MR Garon & EF Storey	1977	Mrs D Henson & JJN Caplan
1946	Miss J Gordon & AA Duncan	1978	Miss T Perkins & R Thomas
1947	Miss J Gordon & AA Duncan	1979	Miss JK Melville & GS Melville
1948	Miss W Morgan & EF Storey	1980	Mrs L Bayman & IW Boyd
1949	Miss F Stephens & LG Crawley	1981	Mrs J Nicolson & NM Stern
1950	Miss F Stephens & LG Crawley	1982	Miss B New & K Dobson
1951	Mrs CA Barclay & G Evans	1983	Miss B New & K Dobson
1952	Mrs RT Peel & GW Mackie	1984	Mrs L Bayman & MC Hughesdon
1953	Miss J Gordon & RG Knipe	1985	Mrs H Kaye & D Longmuir
1954	Miss F Stephens & WA Slark	1986	Miss P Johnson & RN Roderick
1955	Miss P Garvey & PF Scrutton	1987	Mrs J Nicolson & B White
1956	Mrs CA Abrahams & Major WD Henderson	1988	Mrs A Lanrezac & JJN Caplan
1957	Mrs B Singleton & WD Smith	1989	Mrs JM Kershaw & MGA Kershaw
1958	Mrs MF Bonallack & MF Bonallack	1990	Miss S Keogh & A Rogers

Index